SO-BAL-056

TEAMWORK

Douglas Gordon
Career Solutions Training Group
Paoli, PA

VISIT US ON THE INTERNET
www.swep.com
www.thomson.com

South-Western
Thomson Learning™

Cincinnati • Albany, NY • Belmont, CA • Bonn • Boston • Detroit • Johannesburg • London • Madrid
Melbourne • Mexico City • New York • Paris • Singapore • Tokyo • Toronto • Washington

Peter McBride: Business Unit Director
Eve Lewis: Team Leader
Laurie Wendell: Project Manager
Alan Biondi: Editor
Patricia Matthews Boies: Production Manager
Kevin Kluck: Manufacturing Coordinator
Mark Linton: Marketing Manager
Linda Wasserman: Marketing Coordinator

Thanks to the following educators and trainers
who provided valuable assistance during the development of the QUICK SKILLS materials:

Ann K. Jordan
Career Development Manager
Great Oaks Instutute of
Technology and Career Development
Cincinnati, Ohio

Madelyn Schulman
Assistant Director, Career and Occupational Education
Board of Education of the City of New York
Brooklyn, New York

Lyn O'Rourke
Career Services Director
The Academy of Professional Careers
La Mesa, California

Brian Sporleder
Director of Career Services
Bryant and Stratton College
Milwaukee, Wisconsin

Nicola Pidgeon
Coordinator, Business andCommunity Services
Schenectady County Community College
Schenectady, New York

Lori Stearns
Master of Business Administration
Minnesota West Community and Technical College
Jackson, Minnesota

Dr. Doris Humphrey: Project Manager
Jane Galli: Production Editor

CAREER·SOLUTIONS
TRAINING
GROUP

13 East Central Avenue, Paoli, PA 19301
Telephone: 1-888-299-2784 • FAX: (610) 993-8249
E-mail: cstg@bellatlantic.net • Website: www.careersolutionsgroup.com

CONTENTS

When you hear "teamwork," what does it bring to mind? Many people associate teamwork with sports. In athletic events from basketball to soccer, coaches stress the need to put "we" before "I"—the team first, the individual second. Having great players isn't enough to win a championship, the coaches all say. To be successful, the players have to function as a team.

In today's workplaces, the same concept has taken hold. More than ever before, important decisions are being made not by remote, lonely managers but by teams of employees—teams that decide what to do and how to do it. Recently, the Work in America Institute surveyed the leaders of 100 major U.S. companies, asking which skills had the greatest value for their firms. *The number-one answer was teamwork.* These captains of industry considered teamwork more important than traditional problem areas like labor-management relations, training, and recruitment.

Clearly, then, to be successful in a job, you'll need to be good at teamwork. This book will help you learn about the way work teams operate. It will also help you identify and develop the skills you need to be an effective team member—and perhaps a leader. You'll read about topics such as these:

- The nature of teamwork
- Team goals
- The roles that team members play
- The importance of diversity on a team
- Team norms
- Techniques for effective listening and speaking
- How to assert yourself in a team setting
- Handling criticism
- Handling anger and conflict
- Taking appropriate risks
- Developing trust among your teammates
- Solving problems as a team
- Being a team leader

the self-assessment on the next page. For each statement, mark the response that best applies to you.

	Usually	Sometimes	Never
1. I get along well with others in a group.	❏	❏	❏
2. When I'm successful, I'm glad to share the credit with others.	❏	❏	❏
3. I reveal my feelings honestly to others.	❏	❏	❏
4. I speak up to assert my own rights and opinions.	❏	❏	❏
5. I enjoy working with many different types of people.	❏	❏	❏
6. I try to understand why other people think the way they do.	❏	❏	❏
7. I accept criticism gratefully.	❏	❏	❏
8. I resolve conflicts so that everyone benefits.	❏	❏	❏
9. I trust others and expect them to trust me.	❏	❏	❏
10. I'm willing and able to take the lead in a group.	❏	❏	❏

If you checked "Sometimes" or "Never" for any of the above items, you'll find techniques in this book that will help you improve your teamwork skills. Even if you answered "Usually" for all the items, you can use this book to build on your existing talents. Effective teamwork is an area in which all of us can continue to grow.

> " Michael, if you can't pass, you can't play. "
>
> —Legendary basketball coach Dean Smith, speaking to Michael Jordan

On her way to the first team meeting, Natasha hesitates in the hallway, nervous and a little worried.

She has worked in customer service at this insurance company for two years. Along with six others, she answers phone calls and letters from policyholders who have problems. But the policyholders have more questions than she can handle, and often they have to wait for her to get back to them. She's noticed that some of her co-workers have much lighter workloads.

Last week, the department head announced that the unit would be reorganized to improve customer service. Natasha and her co-workers were asked to form a team to work out specific proposals. "You people who actually do the job understand it best," the boss declared, "so the way we reorganize is up to you."

Natasha's one major experience as a team member was with her high school softball team. She thinks a work team must be different, but in what ways? How much extra work, she wonders anxiously, will this team involve? As the youngest person in the department, will she have the nerve to speak up? If she suggests that work be distributed more evenly, will people with lighter workloads resent her? If big changes are made, will she have a lot of new material to learn? And what if the team's ideas don't work—will she take part of the blame?

Well, it's an exciting challenge, she decides—like trying to hit a sinking fastball—and she hurries to the team's first meeting.

What's Inside

In these pages, you will learn to:

The Nature of a Team

Teamwork is a big idea in organizations today. Sooner or later, like Natasha, you'll be asked to work as part of a team.

In a work setting, a *team* is a small group of employees who are working together to achieve a specific goal.
Sometimes the goal is to complete a particular task: for

instance, to create a plan, to recommend options, or to solve a particular problem. In such cases the team is usually temporary, and it will be disbanded once the task is accomplished.

In other cases, the team's goal is to carry out an ongoing function. A team of autoworkers may be in charge of painting each new car that comes off the assembly line. In a hospital a "code" team of nurses and technicians may rush to a patient's room to use emergency life-saving equipment. At a company that makes computer games, a programmer may team with a designer, an artist, and a marketing expert to develop new games. Teams like these are likely to stay together for a long while, and even when individual members are replaced, the team can go on.

The rise of teamwork

Recent decades have brought a special emphasis on teamwork in U.S. organizations. Back in the 1980s, when U.S. manufacturers suffered heavily from imports, analysts wondered why foreign companies were capturing so much of the U.S. market. Often the answer involved the way overseas firms used work teams.

Japanese businesses were especially successful in this respect. In Japan, where teams of employees had the power to make their own decisions, the employees were strongly committed to putting out a high-quality product or service. Two well-known approaches to teamwork, *Total Quality Management (TQM)* and *quality circles*, grew out of study of the Japanese management system.

Today, another phrase you may hear is *self-directed work teams*. This concept, too, relates to the basic notion of organizing employees into teams that have the power to make many of their own decisions.

What decisions do teams make?

Teams are responsible for a wide variety of work-related decisions. Here are some of the decisions that teams often make:

♦ What steps will we take to complete the task?
♦ How will we perform each step?
♦ How will we break down the individual jobs?
♦ Who will be responsible for each job?
♦ What will our schedule be?
♦ How will we monitor our progress?
♦ What will we do if we have problems with the work or the schedule?

My Team Quotient

To judge how ready you are for teamwork in an organization, answer these questions as honestly as you can, using the following scale:

5 Very true of me

4 Often true of me

3 Occasionally true of me

2 Seldom true of me

1 Never true of me

_____ 1. I like solving problems with people in a group.

_____ 2. In a group, I usually let others do the talking.

_____ 3. When people disagree with me, I ask them about their reasoning.

_____ 4. If I have to solve a problem, I prefer to figure it out on my own.

_____ 5. I see myself, at least in some ways, as a potential leader.

_____ 6. If someone contradicts me, I get mad.

_____ 7. When I work with people, I like to set specific goals.

_____ 8. I'm neither a leader nor a follower.

_____ 9. I enjoy having debates and hearing diverse viewpoints.

_____10. When I'm working in a group, I like to know all the rules before we start.

To discover your total score for this activity, first _reverse_ the scores for the even-numbered items. For instance, on item 2, if you wrote a 5, make it a 1; if you wrote a 4, make it a 2. (A 3 stays the same.) Now add up all the numbers. The maximum score is 50. The closer you came to 50, the more likely you are to work well on a team. Whatever your score, however, this book should help you improve your teamwork skills.

Benefits of Teams

From what you've already read, you've gained some idea of why so many people consider teamwork important. But let's look more specifically at the benefits people find in teamwork—first, the typical benefits for the organization, and then the benefits for employees.

Benefits for the organization

From an organization's point of view, many benefits arise from having people work in teams. Compared with the same individuals working on their own, a team provides:

♦ A greater amount of shared knowledge and experience
♦ A wider range of perspectives and insights
♦ More creativity
♦ More critical thinking and high-level thought
♦ Better memory
♦ Greater likelihood that errors will be recognized

♦ Better decision making and problem solving
♦ Greater motivation for the employees involved

And the results of these advantages? There are several obvious ones:

♦ Improved quality of products or services
♦ Improved productivity
♦ Less turnover among employees
♦ Better relationships with customers or clients

> " Two heads are better than one. "
> —Proverb

? Did you know

Work teams often identify and correct problems that cost an organization time and money. At one hospital near Atlanta, a team of employees discovered that much of the IV medication allotted to patients was being wasted. The team managed to decrease the waste by 40 percent.

Similarly, at a General Motors assembly plant, a team focused on the number of cars coming off the assembly line with flat tires. By fixing the problem, the team saved the company about $225,000 a year.

Benefits for team members

What about the team members as individuals? Do they gain as much from teamwork as the organization does?

Typically, the answer is yes. The main reason is the sense of empowerment that team members enjoy.

Empowerment, unfortunately, has become a buzzword. Too many people toss it around in a loose or insincere manner. Still, empowerment is a real phenomenon, and you'll know it when you experience it. Being empowered means that you have feelings like these:

♦ A sense of being able to manage and control your own work.

♦ A conviction that the work really belongs to you—it's more than just a chore you do for somebody else.

♦ A sense of responsibility for the outcome of the work.

Another advantage of teamwork is that it typically allows you to become involved in a larger or wider-ranging job than you would be given on your own. On an old-fashioned assembly line, a worker might spend all day, every day, bolting a tiny doohickey to one corner of each widget that came down the line. As part of a team, that same employee might get involved in all the steps of manufacturing the widget, and perhaps even in redesigning the widget so it would function better. It's immensely more satisfying to work on a whole job than on just a minuscule part.

Teams also are learning experiences for their members. Your team will benefit from the wide range of knowledge, experience, and perspectives that the different members contribute—and so will you. You'll get a chance to learn from the other members. You'll broaden your outlook and enlarge your understanding.

In addition, teams offer important social interactions. They help you develop deeper relationships with a number of your co-workers. Maybe you'll soon be joining other people on your team for refreshments after work. In tough times, your team members may provide much-needed emotional support.

Finally, teams can improve your position within the organization. You can gain status from being part of an important or successful team. And if you demonstrate good skills as a team member, you can enhance your chances of being considered for leadership positions.

What's it like to be empowered?

Empowerment is enjoyable, but it's also challenging.

If your goal is to snooze away your days, with few demands on your time or energy, you don't want to be empowered.

But if you like getting down to work, contributing to a job, and feeling pride in your achievements, then empowerment is one of the best things you can have. It gives you the freedom to make a difference in the world.

A Team of My Own

Think of a team of which you've been a member. You can draw your example from any setting—work, school, religious congregation, volunteerism, or another field. Then answer the following questions about your team:

1. How was working with the team different from working alone?

   _____

   _____

   _____

   _____

   _____

2. In what ways was the team effort similar to working alone?

   _____

   _____

   _____

   _____

   _____

3. What benefits arose from the team members' working together?

   _____

   _____

   _____

   _____

   _____

4. Were there any drawbacks to the team? Explain.

   _____

   _____

   _____

   _____

   _____

What Skills Are Needed?

You may be wondering if unique skills are needed to serve on a work team. The answer is yes and no.

Yes, certain skills are very important. No, they aren't unique skills—they are ones you can apply to all aspects of your life. And you probably have many of these skills already, at least to some degree.

The workshops in this book will help you identify and practice the skills you need for teamwork. Here are some of the major skill categories you'll read about:

♦ Skills in communicating: listening to others, speaking to others, accepting and giving criticism.
♦ Skills in relating to and learning to trust diverse kinds of people.
♦ Skills in being assertive.
♦ Skills in acting with others to resolve conflicts.
♦ Skills in problem solving and decision making.
♦ Skills in leadership.

In skill areas like these, everybody can work for self-improvement. No one ever achieves perfection. Even a famous news anchor can manage to improve her or his communication skills. A chemist who wins the Nobel Prize can learn more about solving problems.

My Skill Priorities

What team-related skills do you most need to develop? Use the following chart to determine your priorities. In the blanks for columns 2 and 3, rate yourself on a scale of 1 to 5, with 5 being the highest. For column 4, add the numbers in columns 2 and 3.

1 Skill Area	2 My Skill Level (1 to 5)	3 Importance to My Career (1 to 5)	4 Priority (add columns 2 and 3)
Listening carefully to others	_____	_____	_____
Accepting criticism without getting angry or defensive	_____	_____	_____
Giving criticism without making others defensive	_____	_____	_____
Accepting and appreciating different kinds of people	_____	_____	_____
Trusting people who are different from me	_____	_____	_____
Managing conflicts	_____	_____	_____
Asserting myself	_____	_____	_____
Controlling my aggressive impulses or anger	_____	_____	_____
Solving complex problems	_____	_____	_____
Being a leader	_____	_____	_____

Which items have the highest priority for you? How will you approach learning more about them?

WORKSHOP WRAP-UP

- A team is a small group of employees working together to achieve a specific goal.
- Teams are increasingly responsible for important decisions in the workplace.
- Teams benefit their individual members as well as the organization as a whole.
- A number of skills are vital for good teamwork, including skills in communication, conflict resolution, and leadership.

2 WORKSHOP

Nick is getting his first chance to design a video game. The company's Slimy Lagoon series has been a huge hit, but only with boys, so a six-person team has been set up to create a new version appealing to girls.

Karen, the company's creative director, is the team leader. At the first meeting she says, "I think we should begin by setting a goal for our team."

"Don't we know what our goal is?" says Tykeisha from Marketing.

"In general, yes," Karen answers, "but we can make it more specific. For instance, are we going to adapt Slimy Lagoon games already in production, or are we building from the ground up? Ideas, anybody?"

"We've got a great game series," says the artist, Pascual, "so can't we just tweak it a little, put in more female characters?"

Jane the scriptwriter speaks up. "I can't help but notice that half our team here is male. And if you guys think that just a few more female characters—drawn like typical male fantasies—are going to make the game appeal to teenage girls, you're out of touch."

"Well, the whole idea," says Max the programmer, "is kind of a male concept, you know. Maybe, no matter what we do, girls won't go for monsters that ooze out of lagoons."

Now Nick chimes in. "But if we scrap the whole concept, what's the point of our team?"

Nick is confused. He feels the team must be starting off on the wrong foot. He looks to Karen, thinking she'll want to set people straight about their purpose. But Karen just leans back in her chair and smiles, letting the discussion go on.

What's Inside

In these pages, you will learn to:

Clarifying Team Goals

As Nick was learning, one of the first steps in establishing a team is for the members to clarify their goals. In Workshop 1, we defined a workplace team as a small group working together toward a specific goal. Without a clear and shared goal, you don't have a team—just a collection of individuals.

Even if supervisors have set up the team for a stated purpose, the members may have different ideas about what that purpose involves. For example, if the team has been asked to recommend changes to improve productivity, members might disagree about what kinds of changes they should consider. If the team is supposed to produce a report, some members might imagine a 10-page report, others a 100-page report.

Clarifying the team's goal means discussing it in the group, letting everyone have some input, and then agreeing on a goal definition that satisfies all the members. The definition doesn't necessarily have to be formal or written down, but a strong sense should develop that everyone is aiming in the same direction.

In some cases this process of clarifying the goal may take just a few minutes. In other cases it may take an entire meeting, or more than one meeting. But if a team skips this step, problems often develop later.

Besides defining the direction the team is heading, the process of clarifying goals has three other important functions:

♦ To help team members see how their individual goals relate to the team's goal
♦ To uncover hidden agendas that some members may have
♦ To build commitment to the team's work and to its outcome

Let's look at each of these three points in turn.

Individual goals and team goals

Each team member enters the group with certain goals of his or her own. These can be conscious or unconscious goals, and they can cover a huge range of possibilities.

> " Every excellent group begins with a dream shared by most members. Group members become keepers of the dream. "
>
> —David W. Johnson and Frank P. Johnson, *Joining Together*

For instance, a group member may want to do any or several of the following:

- Be seen as a leader on the team.
- Earn a promotion.
- Finish with this team as soon as possible and go back to other work.
- Get to know other team members.
- Ask the team leader for a date.
- Use the meeting times to take a welcome rest.
- Learn new skills or information.
- Try new challenges.

Some individual goals will mesh well with the team's overall goal. Others won't. The process of clarifying team goals helps individual members see how to adapt their own desires and intentions to the team effort.

As the team goes on, of course, the individuals may change some of their original goals. Someone who didn't want to be a leader may decide to step forward and take on new responsibilities. A member who wanted to shirk team commitments may discover that the team is well worth the time it takes.

Hidden agendas

Sometimes team members have certain plans in mind for the group. They want the group to follow a particular path. If they try to maneuver the team in that direction without revealing their purpose, we can say that they have *hidden agendas*.

Imagine that your team is selecting a new computer system for the Purchasing Department. The company has always used a Unix operating system, but one team member wants to switch to Linux. Her reason is that she personally dislikes Unix and wants a chance to learn the Linux system. She may be right or wrong in her preference, but this personal agenda of hers doesn't necessarily correspond to what's best for the Purchasing Department or for the company as a whole

Here's another scenario: Last year your company introduced a new product line that was immensely successful. A new team is set up to create spin-off products. The chief designer of last year's line is assigned to the team, but he wants to make sure the spin-offs don't steal any of his glory. If he becomes unhappy with the team's direction, he might find ways to sabotage the project.

The process of clarifying team goals doesn't necessarily reveal all hidden agendas. But it can encourage team members to bring them at least partly to the surface. Once such agendas become known, the team has a much better chance of dealing with them. In our first example, if the team knew about one member's preference for Linux, that could be discussed and evaluated early on. In the second example, the designer could be assured that the team will give him full credit for all his contributions, past and present.

Commitment to the team

Taking time to clarify a team's goal is important for one more reason: It builds the individual members' commitment to the team.

When all members take part in defining the team goal, each member can feel, from the very start, that he or she has contributed to the effort. It's the same effect as when the manager of a baseball team starts a season by making sure that all the players get a chance to play in the first week. Everyone is immediately involved in the group process.

team members all discuss and contribute to the goal, it becomes a kind of personal promise from each member. It's not just a task they have been given; it's something they personally have agreed to do, and they approach the work with greater motivation.

members are committed from the start, they tend to give strong support to the eventual outcome of the team's work. Even if they aren't 100 percent satisfied, they'll generally give the team's effort a vote of confidence. If the team offers a proposal or recommendation, they'll endorse it and recommend that others in the

Did you know

As technology progresses, more and more teams involve people who work in different places—sometimes, even, in different countries. The members "meet" via telecommunications. Groups of this sort are often called *virtual teams*.

E-mail lets people exchange ideas across the world in a matter of seconds. Shared on-line forums allow far-flung team members to comment on a proposal and see what everyone else has said. And improved tools for videoconferencing are making it easier to have a meeting among people who are thousands of miles apart.

My Typical Reactions

Imagine you're placed on a workplace team in which a number of members seem confused about the team's goal and show little commitment to the effort. How would you behave? Use the following scale to assess your likelihood of choosing the various responses:

5 Definitely

4 Probably

3 Maybe

2 Probably not

1 Definitely not

_____ 1. I would ask the group leader to tell us all what we ought to be doing.

_____ 2. I'd get annoyed and refuse to participate.

_____ 3. I'd propose that we all sit down and discuss our goal to make sure we understood it.

_____ 4. I'd tell some of the members they didn't belong on the team.

_____ 5. I would go to the boss and point out the team's ineffectiveness.

_____ 6. Privately, I would ask the group leader if some steps should be taken to bring the group into focus.

_____ 7. I'd work extra hard myself to make up for the slackers.

_____ 8. I'd participate and do what I was asked, but I wouldn't expect the team to accomplish much.

_____ 9. I'd stand up in a meeting and tell everyone what I thought our goals should be.

_____ 10. I'd find ways to ignore or work around the ineffective members.

_____ 11. I'd form my own subgroup that would focus its efforts and accomplish the task.

_____ 12. I'd start looking for another job.

Now look at the reactions that you've rated from 3 to 5. Which of these are best for the team effort? Which are most harmful to the team effort?

_____

_____

_____

Establishing Team Roles

Once a team has agreed on its goal, another early step is to establish the roles that different members will play. A typical team has both formal and informal roles.

Formal roles are stated and explicit responsibilities. They include functions like these:

♦ Leader or chairperson: directs the group's efforts, runs meetings.
♦ Vice chairperson: takes over in the chairperson's absence.
♦ Secretary: records group decisions; takes other notes as necessary; perhaps arranges times and places for meetings.

Often such formal roles are assigned before the team begins its work. For instance, a company executive may appoint the team leader. Sometimes, though, team members have the opportunity to elect people to fill these roles.

Informal roles are ones that members take on for themselves. You may become aware, for instance, that Alida is the team member who takes special responsibility for resolving disagreements. No one has asked her to do so, but she can be counted on to play that role. Tom, on the other hand, is the team cheerleader; whenever morale seems to flag, Tom supplies a pep talk.

Researchers who study organizational teams have given names to a number of common informal roles. Here are a few of those names:

♦ Initiator: often proposes new ideas.
♦ Synthesizer: blends others' ideas together.

♦ Coordinator: often takes the lead in coordinating activities.
♦ Harmonizer: helps resolve disagreements by seeking common ground.
♦ Supporter: praises others' efforts and helps build group solidarity.
♦ Clarifier/summarizer: interprets and summarizes what has been said and done.

Of course, the nature of the informal roles will depend on the type and purpose of the team. Sometimes one individual plays more than one identifiable role. What's important is that the roles combine to make the group function smoothly and efficiently.

Often the need for informal roles will emerge as the group's work progresses. At first, perhaps, no harmonizer is necessary because there aren't any major disputes. But if disagreements arise, someone has to step forward to play the harmonizer role, or the team may get lost in fruitless bickering.

Important roles need people to fill them. Conversely, each person on the team should feel that he or she has a part to play. The strongest work teams are the ones that make best use of what every person can offer.

> " Getting good players is easy. Getting them to play together is the hard part. "
>
> —Casey Stengel

Who's the leader?

In a work group, leadership can take many different forms. You can lead in a formal sense by being the chairperson who directs the team meetings, but you can also lead by playing an informal role that is crucial to the group's success.

For instance, you can be the creative leader—the member who proposes great new ideas. Or you can be the detail person who helps develop and flesh out other people's generalized schemes. You can lead by figuring out how to coordinate the different tasks the group has to do. Or you can lead in a social sense by helping to create a friendly and positive atmosphere.

In Workshop 9 you'll learn more about the many facets of team leadership.

ACTIVITY 2.2

What I Can Bring to a Team

Think about your particular talents and how you could use them to benefit a workplace team. The following questions will help you focus your thoughts.

1. Circle two of the following roles that you think you are best suited to play. Choose your own names for roles if you like.

   Initiator   Synthesizer   Clarifier/summarizer   Supporter   Coordinator   Harmonizer

   Others: _____   _____

2. Explain why you think you'd be good at the first role you circled.

   _____
   _____
   _____
   _____

3. Now explain why you can be successful in the second role.

   _____
   _____
   _____
   _____

What Makes a Good Team?

In addition to a clear, agreed-upon goal and useful roles for all the members, what other characteristics are typical of an effective team? What makes the difference between a team that dazzles and a team that flops?

Nearly all the experts who study organizational teamwork agree that these characteristics are essential:

- An atmosphere of cooperation rather than competition
- Active participation by all members
- Dedication by all to the team's success
- Emphasis on both product and process—that is, on both the task to be done and the teamwork and social skills needed to get it done
- Belief that the team "sinks or swims" together—that all members are interdependent
- Belief that each person is accountable for the success or failure of the group
- Trust among the members
- Encouragement of risk taking and creativity
- Good communication
- Free expression of opinions, with the attitude that disagreement and even occasional conflict are not necessarily bad

- Periodic evaluation of the team's performance by the members themselves, with a willingness to make changes as necessary

In later workshops, you'll read more about these characteristics. The important point here is that an effective team is truly more than the sum of its parts.

Say a group has seven members, and each member can contribute 1 unit of work (however a "unit" is defined). The output of the seven members working alone would amount to 7 units. But working together their total output may be much higher—maybe 20 or 30 units. To achieve this, though, they have to undergo an evolution, changing from seven individuals into something bigger than themselves—a team.

> " We must all hang together, or assuredly we shall all hang separately. "
>
> —Benjamin Franklin

Assessing My Team

1. Focus on a team in which you have participated. Rate it according to the characteristics of an effective team, using a scale of 1 to 5 (with 5 being the highest rating).

Characteristic	Rating (1 to 5)
Atmosphere of cooperation	_____
Active participation by all members	_____
Dedication by all to the team's success	_____
Emphasis on both product and process	_____
Belief that members are interdependent	_____
Belief that each person is accountable	_____
Trust among the members	_____
Encouragement of risk taking and creativity	_____
Good communication	_____
Free expression of opinions	_____
Periodic evaluation of team performance	_____

2. Now add up the total score. _____

3. The maximum possible score is 55. How close did your team come? How does this score correspond with your opinion of the team's effectiveness?

_____

_____

_____

_____

_____

For a somewhat different assessment of a team's characteristics, try Glenn Parker's "Quick Team Check," available on his Web site at

http://www.glennparker.com/Freebees/quick-team-check.html

Or go to the Smart Business Supersite—

http://www.smartbiz.com/

Enter the term *teams* in the search window, and explore some of the articles you find.

WORKSHOP WRAP-UP

- Clarifying the team's goal involves discussing it in the group, letting everyone have input, and then agreeing on a goal definition that satisfies all the members.
- Team roles can be either formal or informal. Through informal roles, every member can play a vital and leading part.
- Characteristics of an effective team include active participation by all members, an atmosphere of cooperation and trust, good communication, and a belief that every member is accountable for the team's performance.

The candy company is building a new plant, and a team of employees will have input into the design. Mei-Ling, a quality checker in Chocolates, is excited about participating.

At the first meeting, Mei-Ling sees that the seven team members range in age from early twenties to late sixties. Five different ethnic groups are represented, including a man from Iran and a woman who grew up in Germany.

In addition, the team members all come from different departments. Herbert is from Accounting, and Mei-Ling's friend Jamilla is from Marketing; then there are people Mei-Ling doesn't know from Hard Candies, Purchasing, Shipping, and Scheduling. In Mei-Ling's experience, these departments have different needs that often lead to squabbles. How will such a mixed team come up with coherent proposals?

The first meeting doesn't reduce Mei-Ling's worries. Herbert from Accounting wants the new plant to have a state-of-the-art computer system; the people in Shipping have detailed requirements for the loading dock; Hard Candies asks for a better temperature-control system.

Everybody wants more space for his or her department, though the new plant won't be much larger than the old one.

After the meeting, Mei-Ling whispers to Jamilla, "Do you think this team is going to work?"

"I think it might," Jamilla says. "Maybe we'll profit from the different points of view. Besides, did you notice that the Iranian looks like a movie star?"

Mei-Ling laughs. Later in the day, thinking about the meeting, she decides that Jamilla is right. If the team can somehow integrate the members' wishes and opinions, the new plant can really become a great place for everyone.

What's Inside

In these pages, you will learn to:

The Benefits of Diversity

As Mei-Ling discovered, workplace teams are often made up of people from very different backgrounds. Often this is true simply because today's workforce is so diverse. If you aren't already working alongside people of different genders, cultures, ethnic groups, ages, and nationalities, you probably will be before long.

But there is another reason for the frequent diversity among team members. Diversity is beneficial. Research on many types of teams, from bankers to bomber crews, has shown that diversity can improve group creativity and decision making. Good managers know this fact, and they keep it in mind when they choose people to serve on teams.

Besides the kinds of diversity already mentioned, managers frequently try to find team members who vary in characteristics such as these:

talents	attitudes
skills	job descriptions
knowledge	working styles
experience	education
personality	social class

"Multiskilled" and "multifunctional" teams—ones that mix people of different skill types and different roles in the organization—are especially prominent in today's businesses.

To understand why diversity is so valuable, imagine a team whose members all think alike, have the same background, and share the same attitudes. The range of choices this team considers will be narrow. There will be little chance for the clash of ideas that stimulates new, original thinking. The group may become stagnant because no one is pushing it to be different. Members will have little to learn from one another. Tasks may arise that no one on the team has skills to handle.

Of course, if diversity becomes too extreme, the team members will struggle to agree on a common goal and to work together. Even in an international company with offices all over the world, you wouldn't want to have a team composed of five people who spoke five different languages and couldn't communicate with one another. Similarly, if differences in personalities are too great, the team may produce more friction than creativity. Managers who set up teams try to find the right balance between similarity and dissimilarity among the team's members.

> " Two heads are better than one only if they contain different opinions.
>
> —Kenneth Kaye, *Workplace Wars and How to End Them*

Diversity on Your Team

Think of a team you've served on, at work, at school, with friends, in athletics, or among your family. Then use the following questions to guide you in thinking about the role of diversity in the team's performance.

1. In what ways was the team diverse? Explain.

    Example: Our high school basketball team had players from three different towns. They were white, Latino, and African American. . . .

    _____

    _____

    _____

    _____

2. What limits were there on the team's diversity? Describe them.

    Example: Everybody was a good shooter, but nobody could play defense.

    _____

    _____

    _____

    _____

3. How do you think your team's overall diversity related to its success?

    _____

    _____

    _____

    _____

    _____

    _____

    _____

    _____

Obstacles to Effective Diversity

To take advantage of the potential benefits of diversity, team members must accept and respect other members who represent different ages, occupations, ethnic groups, and the like. This is a truism, and most of us can readily agree with it. Unfortunately, it's harder to put that belief into practice. Often, even if we think we're being open-minded, we get sidetracked by prejudice or stereotypes.

Prejudice

Prejudice literally means judging in advance—making an evaluation before you've gathered or considered all the relevant information. In a work environment, prejudice operates in subtle ways.

Imagine that you've never been fond of Victoria, who acts like a snob around the office. During a team meeting, Victoria offers to do some research on a particular problem and come up with a proposal for handling it. Maybe, you suppose, she's volunteering in order to impress the team leader and earn brownie points. At the next meeting, when Victoria describes what she's learned and offers a recommendation for action, you're dubious. You see a couple of flaws in her idea—not major flaws, but you figure there must be other problems as well. In the group discussion, therefore, you oppose her proposal. Partly because of your opposition, the team decides to go in another direction.

In this scenario you may be showing prejudice. That is, because of your dislike for Victoria, you may have judged her proposal before you considered it fully. If, in fact, the proposal was good, you've helped steer the team in the wrong direction.

There are many other potential reasons for prejudice, including emotions such as fear, anger, and jealousy. Prejudice is most likely to influence our opinions of people who are very different from us. That is why prejudice can be a great hindrance for a diverse work team.

Did you know

One frequent source of prejudice is our own first impressions. How can that be? Typically, once we form an impression of someone, we pay attention to further information that confirms what we already think, but we ignore information that contradicts it.

For instance, if you decide on your first day at work that your boss is mean, the boss may do a hundred nice things over the next year without changing your opinion.

The way to counter this tendency is to make a conscious effort to keep learning about other people even when you think you've got them "pegged."

Stereotypes

A *stereotype* is a belief that certain groups of people tend to have distinct characteristics. In other words, it's an assumption that belonging to a certain group will make a person look, think, or act in a particular way.

You may think you're free from stereotypes, but you're not. We all rely on stereotypes every day. Often, because we know little about a person as an individual, we have to depend on what we know (or think we know) about the groups he or she belongs to. Imagine, for instance, that on December 24 many people you work with have been greeting each other with the phrase "Merry Christmas!" You've been using that phrase as well. However, when you pass Yusuf in the cafeteria, you decide not to say that. You know that Yusuf is from Saudi Arabia, so you suppose he's a Muslim and doesn't celebrate Christmas. Because you have nothing else to go on, you're relying on a stereotype about people from Saudi Arabia with Arabic-sounding names.

That way of using a stereotype is usually benign. Often, in fact, it helps you avoid causing unnecessary offense. But now imagine a different scenario:

At a team meeting, a young employee proposes a revolutionary new idea for solving a problem. On the surface it sounds great. Then an older team member, who always dresses in a dark blue suit and red tie and has been with the company a long time, points out some problems with the proposal and suggests a more cautious approach. Your first reaction may be that the older member is a stick-in-the-mud, someone who will oppose any innovation just because it's new. Maybe your reaction is correct, maybe not. The problem is that it may be based on a negative, unjustifiable stereotype. You may be assuming that older people are always timid and afraid of change, or that men who wear dark blue suits are always stuffy and conservative. In that case your use of a stereotype becomes a type of prejudice and distorts your judgment.

The Seven Deadly Isms

Psychologist Kenneth Kaye has identified what he calls the "seven deadly isms" that damage relationships and teamwork within organizations. They are:

♦ Sexism
♦ Elitism
♦ Racism
♦ Favoritism
♦ Ageism
♦ Individualism
♦ Chauvinism

In your own experience, which of these is the most "deadly"? Why do you think so?

Combating Prejudice and Stereotypes

No one is completely free from prejudice or negative stereotypes. But everyone can reduce their harmful impact by making a conscious effort. Here are some useful suggestions to remember:

♦ Be conscious of the assumptions you're making about people.

♦ When you form an opinion about a person or idea, make sure you have thought it through. Honestly examine your own reasoning.

♦ Always keep yourself open to new information about other individuals.

♦ Take opportunities to learn more about groups of which you have little knowledge.

♦ Remember that every person is unique.

ACTIVITY 3.2

Dealing with Stereotypes

Recall an incident of harmful stereotyping that you have observed. It might be one in which you were either the perpetrator or the victim.

1. What false assumption(s) was the stereotyper making about the individual?

_____

_____

_____

2. What false assumption(s) was the stereotyper making about the group to which the individual belonged?

_____

_____

_____

3. What steps could the stereotyper have taken to avoid making these errors? Be as specific as possible.

_____

_____

_____

4. Could the victim of stereotyping have taken any steps to avoid the problem? Explain.

_____

_____

_____

Quick Skills

You can use the resources of the World Wide Web to break down some of your own stereotypes. Choose a significant group about which you have definite feelings but relatively little knowledge: surfers, vegans, rappers, Unitarians—nearly any such group should have some presence on the Web. Use a Web directory or search engine to find listings of sites that cater to members of the group. For example, you can go to the Yahoo! home page at

http://www.yahoo.com/

and follow the links for "Society & Culture," then "Cultures and Groups." Examine some of the sites you find, and then assess what you have learned. Does your additional information about the group change your opinion of it? Will you think differently about that group in the future?

Making Diversity Work

When you join a diverse team, you'll want to maximize the benefits that diversity offers. But besides controlling your own prejudices and stereotypes, what else can you do to help the team benefit from the talents and perspectives of all its members?

Here are several steps you can take regardless of your position on the team—whether you're a formal leader or not:

♦ Make a point of being flexible and adaptive in the way you approach the team process, understanding that other people may want to work in different ways than you normally do.

♦ Make an effort to associate with team members of different backgrounds and different points of view. Chat with them after meetings. Go out to lunch with them.

♦ In team interactions, solicit the input of people who might otherwise be excluded.

♦ Act as a bridge between members who are "like" you and others who are "different." Help clarify miscommunications and misunderstandings between them. Find ways to integrate their different approaches.

♦ Be careful and sensitive in your use of language (see the feature "Watch Your Word Choice!").

♦ Show that you can change your mind if someone presents a better argument than yours.

♦ Encourage honest expression of both ideas and feelings.

Watch your word choice!

Some terms describing race, ethnic group, gender, and so on are clearly derogatory, and most people know to avoid them. Often, though, people get in trouble by using words they think are innocent. Look at these examples:

girl	Any female old enough to be working with you probably doesn't want to be called a girl.
lady	Even an older, traditional female may prefer to be called a woman.
gal(s)	Possibly offensive to any female.
boy	Offensive when used for any male old enough to be working with you.
Indian	Acceptable in referring to someone from India, but possibly offensive to a Native American.
Chicano	Preferred by some Mexican Americans, disliked by others.
Hispanic	Potentially offensive when it shows a failure to distinguish among different nationalities; even as a general classification, some may prefer *Latino/Latina*.
black	Some may prefer *African American*; some may not.
colored	Though still used for people of mixed heritage in South Africa, this term is generally considered offensive in the United States.
Oriental	Often taken as derogatory.
Asian	Acceptable as a very generic term; offensive when it fails to distinguish Chinese from Koreans, East Asians from South Asians, and so on.
Hebrew	Name of a language, but often derogatory when used for a person.
cripple	No longer courteous for a person with a disability.
handicap	Often less favored than *disability*.

Such examples could go on forever. Since the accepted language changes over time, you need to be sensitive to evolution in terminology. This doesn't mean that you have to be so politically correct that you refer to a short person as "vertically challenged." Keep in mind, though, that the language you use—and the language you encourage others on your team to use—may have a strong impact on your ability to work together.

So You Think That's Funny?

Think of a joke you've heard that depends on stereotypes about a particular group for its humor—an ethnic or racial group, occupational group, age group, gender group, or any other kind of group. When you have your joke in mind, answer the following questions about it.

1. What characteristics does your joke assume are shared by all members of the group?

    _____

    _____

2. If you were a member of the group, and someone told the joke in your presence, would you be offended? Why or why not?

    _____

    _____

3. How often do you hear or tell such jokes? Circle one answer.

    Frequently   Occasionally   Never

4. Do you think you and/or the people around you need to modify the use of such jokes? Explain.

    _____

    _____

    _____

    _____

WORKSHOP WRAP-UP

- Diverse membership helps teams become creative and make better decisions.
- For a diverse team to be effective, members need to combat prejudice and stereotypes.
- To make diversity work, team members should be flexible, associate with others of different backgrounds, choose their language with care, and encourage participation and honest communication by all.

Katrina sees herself as a solidarity-builder. Nobody gave her that job, but she frequently does little things that help maintain cohesiveness among the six people on her team. For instance, when somebody has a birthday, she collects contributions for a cake, a card, and a small present. When they're all working hard to meet a deadline, she'll be the one who yells, "We're ordering pizza! Who wants pepperoni?" Last month, she arranged a Saturday picnic and softball game for team members and their families.

The team's function is to test and repair hard drives for the company's factory-rebuilt computers. The team is allowed to set its own work procedures, and the members really do blend together well— except for Len. Though he may be their most skilled member, Len seems to hold back from committing himself to the team.

For instance, when the team has meetings to review the work, Len doesn't seem to listen to other people's remarks; he acts bored and impatient. At lunchtime he usually goes off by himself, not talking to others. He skipped the picnic, too. And last week, when the five others decided to stay late to finish an important order, Len had to be coaxed. "I was going to a movie tonight," he grumped. "I do have my own life, you know."

Some of these matters are trivial, Katrina tells herself, but she sees that other team members have begun to avoid Len whenever possible. Team morale is suffering.

Katrina decides to act. One day, she draws Len out to the hallway. "Can you spare me a minute, Len? There's something I'd like to talk about with you."

What's Inside

In these pages, you will learn to:

Committing Versus Conforming

What do you think Katrina will say to Len? How can she explain the problem?

Len may not realize his behavior is troublesome. After all, as far as job tasks are concerned, he is performing excellently.

Moreover, in our society we tend to value individualism. We admire people who "march to a different drummer." We look down on conformists. Somebody who always goes along with the group may be labeled a "sheep" or worse.

Somehow Katrina needs to convey to Len that a good team member must do more than just show up and perform the job. He should commit to the group in a deeper sense. But this doesn't mean sacrificing his individuality.

In this workshop you'll investigate what commitment to a team really means. Keep the story of Len and Katrina in mind, because in the last activity you'll be asked to describe what you would say to Len if you took Katrina's place.

The Team Effort

In Workshop 2 you learned the importance of discussing and clarifying team goals. By giving everyone a chance to have input, this process increases members' motivation to help the team.

Still, there is no magic formula for winning everyone's commitment. It is each member's responsibility to accept the team goal and devote the time and energy necessary to realize it. This is easier to say than to do. If you disagree with some of the team's basic choices, or if you harbor some deep-seated worries about the nature of teamwork, you may find yourself hanging back from full commitment.

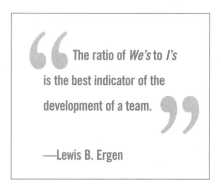

> " The ratio of *We's* to *I's* is the best indicator of the development of a team. "
>
> —Lewis B. Ergen

What if you disagree with the team?

If the team follows a direction that you approve, you'll probably be eager to contribute as much as you can. But imagine the opposite situation. You advocate Plan A, but the team adopts Plan B, and your feelings are hurt because you think other members should have paid more attention to you. You may be tempted to react in one or more of the following ways:

♦ Sulk and refuse to contribute.
♦ Go along on the surface, but do as little work as possible.
♦ Hope that Plan B fails so that other team members will see how smart you were to oppose it.
♦ At each meeting, remind the team that you disagree with the basic approach.
♦ Actively sabotage the work.

Needless to say, responses like these are damaging to the team. To be an effective team member, you need to commit yourself fully to making Plan B work, even if you originally disagreed with it. If Plan B then fails despite your best efforts, you can step forward again with your own proposal.

Of course, if the team adopts a goal or plan that you feel is outrageous—for instance, an approach that will harm others, damage the organization, or violate ethical rules—you can't be expected to bend your conscience to participate. Your first responsibility is to argue as strongly as you can against that approach. If the team insists on it anyway, you should resign from the team and perhaps alert your superiors.

Your attitude toward the team

Even though you understand the benefits of teamwork, you may have a number of worries about the operation of a team. Especially in the early stages of a team's development, people often have concerns like these:

♦ Other people will loaf, and I'll get stuck with more than my share of the work.
♦ I'll be blamed for what goes wrong.
♦ I won't get enough credit for my contributions.
  ♦ I'll waste my time listening to other people meander.
  ♦ Popularity, not intelligence, will rule.
  ♦ The loudest voices will rule.
  ♦ I'll be expected to go along with other people's crazy plans.
  ♦ While I'm working for this team, my real job will suffer.

These worries are not silly. Each of them focuses on a problem that some teams actually face. But if you allow concern about them to undermine your commitment to the team, you may be creating a self-fulfilling prophecy: that is, the team may fail partly because you expected it to fail.

A better option is to try to keep a good attitude. Say to yourself, "This team is going to succeed. I'm going to help it succeed. Whatever problems we have, we can work out along the way."

? Did you know

In the 1920s a French professor of agricultural engineering, Max Ringelmann, investigated the most efficient way of pushing or pulling a load. He experimented with teams of people, oxen, and machinery.

As part of his study, he attached a rope to a pressure gauge and asked people to pull on it. He tried individuals, groups of two people, groups of three, and groups of eight. What do you think he found?

The larger groups did pull harder than the smaller groups. But eight people didn't pull nearly eight times as hard as one person. These were the comparative results:

2 people	1.87 times as hard as 1 person
3 people	2.54 times as hard as 1 person
8 people	3.94 times as hard as 1 person

In other words, the more people were added to the group, the less average effort each individual put out! Later researchers found the same pattern—dubbed the Ringelmann effect—in many other types of groups.

Another name given to this kind of behavior is *social loafing*. What do you think a team can do to combat it?

What Keeps You from Commitment?

Think about your own history of teamwork and your typical level of commitment to a team. Then answer the following questions.

1. What are your own common worries about being a member of a team?

   _____

   _____

   _____

   _____

   _____

2. How do these worries affect your attitudes toward the team and your commitment to the team's work?

   _____

   _____

   _____

   _____

   _____

3. Could you be a more effective team member if you changed your attitudes? (Circle one answer.)

                   Yes   No

4. If you answered "Yes" to question 3, what specifically can you do to change your attitudes?

   _____

   _____

   _____

   _____

   _____

Team Norms

On Saturday mornings, the crew team has an early-morning workout on the river, and afterward the members pile into a car and head to a local diner for breakfast. There, while wolfing down huge stacks of pancakes, they talk about their progress, trade suggestions, tease each other, set informal goals for the coming week, and generally reinforce their solidarity as a team.

Eating pancakes in the diner is not a

formal requirement for membership on this team. But if one member regularly skips the breakfast, his or her commitment to the team can be questioned. That person may be seen as an outsider, not a full member of the group, and perhaps not completely trustworthy. Fair or not, such opinions are likely to arise whenever a member violates a team norm.

A *norm* is any behavior or attitude that a group considers appropriate for its members. Norms can take many different forms. Here are a few examples:

◆ *Team norms that echo norms in the wider society.* In a meeting, for instance, people are expected to speak in turn, not interrupting others. This is a typical norm throughout our society, and it will apply in nearly every group to which you belong.

◆ *Team norms that represent an extension or interpretation of wider social norms.* In every organization, people are expected to come to meetings on time. But if a

particular team regularly meets at 3:00, it may become clear that the first ten minutes are for socializing and assembling, and therefore a busy member can arrive at 3:09 without being considered late. In this way the team modifies the norm of promptness to suit its own needs.

◆ *Team norms that are unique to that group.* Attendance at the crew team's Saturday pancake breakfast is an example of a unique norm that one particular group evolved. Unique team norms may involve certain rituals, ways of speaking, or any other kind of behavior that the group comes to treat as normal and expected.

Most team norms are not formally stated. They simply evolve over time as the team develops a shared sense of what is suitable.

As a team member, you'll play a part in establishing the group's norms. You'll also be expected to follow those norms yourself. And when another team member violates a norm, you may be expected to join in "correcting" that wayward soul. Maybe, for example, you'll find yourself speaking to another team member in private, explaining why his or her behavior is causing discontent among the other members.

Activity 4.2 will help you apply these concepts to your own experience.

Violating a Norm

Reflect on a time when a teammate of yours (or perhaps you yourself) violated a team norm. Answer the following questions about the experience.

1. What was the norm that the person violated? Was it stated openly or just assumed?

    _____

    _____

    _____

2. How well do you think the member understood the norm he or she was violating?

    _____

    _____

    _____

3. What sanctions (penalties or punishments) did the team direct toward the offending member? Which people did the sanctioning?

    _____

    _____

    _____

4. Were the sanctions effective? Why or why not?

    _____

    _____

    _____

5. What could the team have done to reduce the chances that someone would violate this norm?

    _____

    _____

    _____

Listening to Others

Another aspect of committing to the team is making the effort to listen carefully to what other team members have to say. Too often, we listen superficially—that is, we seem to be paying attention, but our minds are drifting. Psychologists have discovered that in a typical conversation, even with just one other person, we alternate between "tuning in" and "tuning out." The problem is that, while we're tuned out, we may miss a lot of information.

If your friend is telling you about a movie she saw, it may not matter that your mind drifts a bit. For teamwork, though, effective listening is very important. Even if you think certain team members have nothing worthwhile to say, you can't really collaborate with them until you listen. When you do listen, you may find that they have more to offer than you suspected. At least, by listening, you'll learn more about their attitudes and preferences, and that knowledge can help you win their acceptance of your own proposals.

In his book 7 *Survival Skills for a Reengineered World*, William Yeomans lists nine reasons why people in work situations often don't listen:

1. Your mind does not like to pay attention.
2. You think faster than people talk.
3. People are boring.
4. You rehearse your responses while people talk.
5. You have too much on your mind.
6. Listening puts you in a "second-class" role.
7. You think the speaker is a loser.
8. You don't believe much anyone tells you anyway.
9. You can't hear.

To combat such problems and listen more effectively, you can use active listening techiniques. See the discription of these techniques on the next page.

> **Give every man thy ear, but few thy voice.**
>
> —William Shakespeare

GETTING CONNECTED

For further ideas about improving your listening skills, explore the Web site of the International Listening Association, especially the sections called "Listening Exercises" and "Quotes about Listening." You can find the association at

http://www.listen.org/

Active listening techniques

Active listening means what the phrase implies: you approach listening in an active rather than passive way. Active listening techniques include these:

Attending	Focusing closely on the speaker and maintaining eye contact.
Paraphrasing	Repeating what the speaker has said in your own words, giving him or her an opportunity to correct you if you have misunderstood: "You're saying that the plan is too expensive, is that it?"
Summarizing	Offering an occasional summary of the main points made so far: "Let's see, you've mentioned three points . . ."
Interpretation checking	Stating your interpretation of what the speaker is conveying—both ideas and feelings—and asking if you're correct: "It sounds like you're upset that we aren't beginning with a cost analysis, is that right?"
Using clarifying questions	Asking questions that attempt to make a point clearer or more explicit: "What kind of cost analysis do you think we should be doing?"
Using probing questions	Asking questions that encourage the other person to expand or elaborate on what was said: "I think I know generally what your point is, but can you explain it further?"

Simply knowing these techniques isn't enough. You need to practice them regularly in your team environment. Besides improving your understanding of others, active listening has another important effect: It provides a good example for other team members, so that when your turn comes to speak, they'll be more inclined to listen to you!

A Talk with Len

Look back at the scenario at the beginning of this workshop. Pretend that you, instead of Katrina, are the one who must speak to Len about his contribution to the team. On the lines below, write what you will say to him, considering all that you've learned in this workshop.

_____

_____

_____

_____

_____

_____

_____

_____

_____

_____

WORKSHOP WRAP-UP

- Committing to a team means accepting the team's goals and devoting the time and energy necessary to realize them, even if you don't agree with all the team's decisions.
- Team norms are behaviors and attitudes that the group considers appropriate for its members. All members help create the norms, and all are expected to follow them.
- Willingness to listen carefully to other team members is an important aspect of team commitment.

5 WORKSHOP

Raoul works at a large home-and-garden center. Recently many customers have complained about advertised items that are out of stock, and Raoul has been asked to join a team to investigate the problem.

At the first meeting, somebody from Receiving discussed the process of unloading delivery trucks, adding items to the computerized inventory records, and so on. Now, during the second meeting, the team leader asks for suggestions to speed up the Receiving operations.

Raoul has a different focus on the problem. He spends much of his time stocking the shelves. The other day, after he'd spent two hours with paint cans in aisle 16, he noticed that the shelves of lawn chairs in aisle 23—chairs advertised at a special price—were empty. When he returned to the stockroom, he saw a new shipment of chairs ready to be shelved, with no one attending to them.

What the store needs, Raoul thinks, is a way to prioritize the stocking operation. But how can he introduce this idea when the team seems to be heading in a different direction? Will the senior team members listen to him? Will his supervisor get mad if he hears that Raoul has criticized the stocking process?

Finally, toward the end of the meeting, Raoul cautiously signals with his hand. "Um," he says, "next time, or sometime, could we talk about the way we stock the shelves? I mean, that's what I do, stocking, and I have some ideas about it."

All eyes turn to Raoul, making him blush. His mouth is dry and his palms are sweating. But the team leader beams and says, "Sure, Raoul, thanks, we'll put that on the agenda."

What's Inside

Expressing Yourself

Like Raoul, many of us have difficulty speaking up in a meeting or other team situation, especially when we feel that others may be more knowledgeable or experienced than we are. But committing to the team—being a full-fledged contributor—requires getting up the gumption to make our own ideas heard.

Did you know

About 10 million Americans have such severe shyness that their condition is considered a psychological illness. This "social anxiety disorder," as it is formally known, is the nation's third most widespread mental health problem, following depression and substance abuse.

Expressing yourself is the flip side of good listening, and it is just as important. Remember what you read in Workshop 3 about the value of diversity. On any team, you are part of that diversity, and your opinions and insights are important to the team process. Only you can contribute what's inside your head. Even if you don't have the answer to a particular problem, your comments may inspire other members to develop an answer.

But what can you do if, like Raoul, you become terribly self-conscious about speaking? Four steps can help you conquer this problem:

Step 1: Identify the reasons for your shyness. Ask yourself what you're afraid of. Are you worried that you'll look foolish in front of your co-workers? That the boss will think you're ill-informed? That people will notice your bad haircut?

Step 2: *Use logic to refute your worries.* Logic will tell you, for example, that you're not likely to sound any more foolish than others, and even if you do make a remark that's not 100 percent right, that merely puts you in the same category as everyone else. Other team members can't expect you to be perfect.

Step 3: *Keep your "self-talk" positive.* Self-talk consists of the characteristic things you say silently to yourself about your performance. A shy person often mentally repeats phrases like "I'm going to sound really stupid" and "They're all going to stare at me." Instead of such negative, discouraging thoughts, keep at the front of your mind the truths your logical analysis has identified: "My ideas are as good as anyone else's," "I do know what I'm talking about because of my own experience," and so forth.

Step 4: *Practice, practice, practice.* Each time you speak up and express your ideas, the next time will become a little easier. Gradually you'll develop more confidence, and you'll also gain social skills that help you speak readily in groups. For example, you'll learn how to break into a rapid-flowing conversation without interrupting someone else. You'll discover ways to signal that you have something to say (clearing your throat, gesturing, perhaps nodding your head vigorously). Your timing will improve.

> "Trust yourself. You know more than you think you do.
>
> —Dr. Benjamin Spock

Quick Skills

Assessing Your Shyness

The following questions will help you assess your difficulties with shyness and identify ways to conquer them.

1. In what situations do you have the most trouble overcoming shyness? Check all that apply.

   _____ Around people I don't know   _____ Around people with authority

   _____ In large groups   _____ In small groups

   _____ Around the opposite sex   _____ When somebody asks me for a comment

   _____ When I'm not the leader   _____ When I'm expected to be a leader

   Other situations (specify):

   _____ _____   _____ _____

2. What do you think are the main reasons for your shyness in these situations? Check all that apply.

   _____ Fear of being judged harshly   _____ Fear of attracting attention

   _____ Fear of not being taken seriously   _____ Fear that I'll be inarticulate

   _____ Fear that I'll say the wrong thing   _____ Fear of starting an argument

   Other situations (specify):

   _____ _____   _____ _____

3. How can you apply the four steps for overcoming shyness described in the preceding section? Be as specific as possible.

   _____

   _____

   _____

   _____

   _____

Assertiveness Versus Aggressiveness

Often the way you express yourself is as important as what you have to say. To promote good teamwork, your goal should be to assert yourself, not to be aggressive about your opinions.

What's the difference, you may wonder, between assertiveness and aggressiveness? Don't both mean speaking up firmly, staking your claim to be heard, and arguing for what you believe in? Yes, but an assertive approach respects the ideas and feelings of others. An aggressive approach, in contrast, takes no account of whether other people may be wounded by what you say.

Imagine that you disagree with a plan that Wally has put forth. You could break in and say, "That's wrong. I have a better idea. Listen, here's the right way to do it." This is an aggressive response. It shows disrespect for Wally's idea and challenges his self-esteem. As a result, it may alienate Wally and provoke conflict in the team.

Instead of aggression, you could use assertiveness. You could wait until Wally finishes and then say, "Wally, you've made some good points, but consider this alternative." This response puts your proposal into play without belittling Wally. By showing respect for him, you invite respect for yourself as well.

Some specific techniques can help you assert yourself without being aggressive:

- Direct eye contact
- Posture that is firm and straight but not stiff
- Serious but not severe facial expressions
- Gestures that reinforce the message without threatening
- Objective (not judgmental) language
- Short, to-the-point sentences
- Honest statements of feelings and desires
- Voice that is steady and strong without being loud
- Demonstrated respect for other people's opinions

Learning assertiveness, like overcoming shyness, requires practice. But each time you assert yourself, you build confidence for the next time.

> " Unfortunately, too many people confuse aggressiveness with assertiveness. "
>
> —Rudolph Verderber

Practice Your Assertiveness

Imagine the following situation: Your team is working on a big project. At the start of the work, you had what you knew was an excellent plan, but the team chose another direction, mostly because the team leader, Bruce, insisted on his own opinion while discounting yours. Now the team's in trouble, and you think you must come to the rescue by putting your own plan forward once again. At a team meeting, various people are sitting around complaining about the lack of progress, though Bruce insists everything is okay. You clear your throat and begin to speak.

On the lines below, sketch out what you will say. Include notes about your tone of voice, your gestures, and so on.

_____

_____

_____

_____

_____

_____

Seizing Opportunities

In Workshop 2 you learned that a typical team has a number of informal roles for its members. Some people, for instance, become initiators, the ones who frequently propose new ideas. Others become synthesizers (blending ideas) or harmonizers (resolving disagreements). The variety of informal roles allows everyone to be a leader in some sense.

To become a full-fledged contributor to your team, you need to identify the roles you can play and use them to make an impact. You aren't on the team just to occupy space. To employ your unique talents to best advantage, you need to seize opportunities to contribute to the team effort.

Here are some common ways in which even a new and relatively inexperienced team member can make an impact:

♦ Look for new ways to use your talents and your energy, and volunteer whenever you can.
♦ Share all important information and opinions with other team members. (Don't keep secrets.)
♦ Be honest about your thoughts and feelings.
♦ Complete your own assignments thoroughly and on time.

- Assist other team members who need help.
- Show your dedication to the team goal.
- Help encourage all team members to participate.
- Help create a friendly but productive team environment.
- Work to resolve conflicts constructively (see Workshop 6 for suggestions).
- Share credit with others when things go well.
- Praise others for their contributions.
- Accept your fair share of blame when problems arise.

One other important way to contribute deserves special mention. To help the team progress, you need to stay flexible and encourage others to do the same. In this context, flexibility doesn't mean being able to touch your toes. Rather, it means being open to new ideas, listening carefully to viewpoints that may be strange to you, and showing a willingness to try methods and procedures you've never used before. After all, the point of a team is to blend the inputs of different people to achieve what none could have achieved alone. If you act rigid, refusing to change your cherished way of doing things, you can't very well blend with the team.

Ten quick ways to undermine a team

1. Associate with only the team members you like and snub the others.
2. Keep important information to yourself, refusing to share it.
3. Tell nasty stories about other team members.
4. Find fault with everyone else's ideas, so that all your feedback is negative.
5. Get angry when someone disagrees with you.
6. Refuse to examine your own biases.
7. Ignore the group norms.
8. Slack off on your assignments, assuming other people will do the work.
9. Blame other team members when things go wrong.
10. Claim personal credit for everything that goes right.

Identifying Areas for Improvement

In order to identify some team-building skills on which you need to concentrate, rate yourself with the following chart. For each skill listed, place a check mark on the appropriate line.

My Current Skill Level

	Good	Mediocre	Terrible
1. Doing my work on time	_____	_____	_____
2. Sharing my knowledge with teammates	_____	_____	_____
3. Volunteering	_____	_____	_____
4. Showing that I appreciate other's work	_____	_____	_____
5. Sharing credit and blame	_____	_____	_____
6. Helping to create a friendly environment	_____	_____	_____
7. Encouraging all members to participate	_____	_____	_____
8. Being flexible in thinking and procedures	_____	_____	_____

Now, for each skill that you didn't mark "Good," list specific things you can do to start your progress toward improvement:

Skill No.	What I Can Do
1	*Set a reasonable work schedule for each task and stick to it.*
_____	_____
_____	_____
_____	_____
_____	_____
_____	_____
_____	_____

GETTING CONNECTED

For a measure of your assertiveness, try the Assertiveness Test provided by QueenDom.Com, available at either of these two Web sites:

http://www.psychtests.com/

http://www.queendom.com/

Or look at the questionnaire on assertiveness offered by the Self Renewal Group in London, available at

http://www.srg.co.uk/assertiveness.html

WORKSHOP WRAP-UP

- Expressing yourself is just as important to the team as good listening.
- If you're shy about speaking up, four steps can help: identifying the reasons, using logic to refute your worries, keeping your self-talk positive, and taking every opportunity to practice these skills.
- Asserting yourself requires speaking up firmly, staking your claim to be heard, arguing for what you believe, and at the same time showing respect for others' ideas.
- A genuine team contributor seizes opportunities to use his or her talents: for example, by volunteering for assignments, assisting other team members who need help, and encouraging all to participate.

6 WORKSHOP

Miguel is hot under the collar. A nurse at a geriatric hospital, he is serving on a team that is supposed to develop a new way of scheduling the staff's work hours. Many of the nurses have complained about being required to work some night or weekend shifts. They don't have enough quality time with their families, they say, and switching back and forth from day to night shifts exhausts them.

Miguel often gets tired, too. Personally, though, he likes the flexibility of the current system. His fiancée, a flight attendant, is away several days a week. When she's home, he spends a lot of time with her, but when she's out of town, he volunteers for extra shifts to earn overtime.

At the first team meeting, Miguel felt his opinions were ignored by those who were pushing for a system of fixed hours. One nurse especially, Samantha, got on his nerves. Four separate times, she complained about missing her children's Saturday soccer games, as if that were the biggest tragedy anybody could face.

At today's meeting, when she utters the same lament, Miguel snaps at Samantha. "Listen," he says, "the world doesn't revolve around you and your kids. You're not paying attention to other people's needs."

"And what are your needs, Mister Bachelor?" she snaps back. "More quality time to drink beer and watch football?"

"Wait a minute," says Natalie, the senior nurse on the team. "We can find a way to solve this conflict, but not if we start abusing each other. How about if we list all the issues involved and go over them one by one?"

What's Inside

In these pages, you will learn to:

Constructive Versus Destructive Conflict

In the scenario you've just read, Miguel and Samantha had different goals. Miguel thought Samantha was blocking his goals of keeping the work hours flexible. Similarly, Samatha believed Miguel might prevent her from spending weekends with her children. This is the basis of conflict—when two goals collide.

On any team, conflict can be destructive. It can prevent team members from cooperating to reach the larger team goal. If one party "wins" and the other "loses," the losers may not support the team's eventual recommendations. In the worst cases, conflict can create so much hostility that the team falls apart, and in this case everybody loses because the team is seen as a failure.

Many times, however, conflict can be useful and constructive. In Workshop 3 you learned that diversity of opinions and backgrounds can make a team stronger. Conflict, if handled right, can operate in the same way. After all, if two goals appear to be incompatible, the team needs to deal with that fact rather than paper it over. Conflict can stimulate the team to come up with creative ideas that resolve the seemingly incompatible goals and improve the situation for everyone.

What makes a conflict constructive rather than destructive? The following conditions help ensure that a conflict becomes constructive:

♦ The problem is seen as a mutual problem. In other words, neither party says, "I'm okay, *you're* the one with a problem."

♦ The parties pursue a "win-win" outcome, in which both parties gain, rather than a "win-lose" strategy in which one person has to lose in order for the other to win.

♦ Both people express their ideas openly and communicate effectively.

♦ Each person takes the other seriously and treats him or her with respect.

♦ Both people feel they have influenced the outcome.

In the rest of this workshop, you'll learn some techniques that can help you make conflicts constructive.

> " Conflict itself is neither good nor bad. . . . What matters about conflict, in the end, is how we respond to it. "
>
> —Brian Muldoon, *The Heart of Conflict*

Giving and Receiving Criticism

Harmful conflicts often flare when team members criticize one another. In many cases the person being criticized becomes defensive and angry. That's only natural. None of us likes to be criticized.

Obviously, though, a team can't solve the problem of hurt feelings by refraining from all criticism. If nobody on the team utters a critical word, the team can't separate good ideas from poor ones. Team members need to be free to say what they think, even when they disagree.

To make criticism constructive rather than destructive, team members need two key sets of skills: skills for receiving criticism, and skills for giving it.

Skills for receiving criticism

Too often, when someone criticizes us, we don't even really listen. We react with immediate defensive measures. For instance, we throw an insult back at the other person, or we stomp away, furious. As a result, if there is any truth in the person's critique—as there often is—we fail to benefit from it. Rather than use the critique to improve our contribution to the team, we turn it into an occasion for divisiveness.

The following four steps can help you improve the way you receive criticism:

Step 1: Put aside your ego as much as possible. Separate your inner self from the criticism. If you receive criticism about a particular task, remind yourself that only that task is in question, not your overall performance—and certainly not your worth as a human being.

Step 2: Suspend judgment about what you hear. Don't decide immediately whether the other person is right or wrong. Wait until you have a chance to think it over.

Step 3: Listen hard to the advice itself—the information contained in the message. Concentrate fully on what the speaker is telling you so that you understand what the criticism is really about.

Step 4: Use active listening techniques—that is, take an active role in the conversation to make sure you've understood. As described in Workshop 4, active listening techniques include attending, paraphrasing, summarizing, interpretation checking, and using clarifying and probing questions.

Skills for giving criticism

Just as the person being criticized should avoid getting defensive, the person offering the critique has a responsibility for phrasing it in a constructive way. That sounds easy enough to do, but how exactly do you accomplish it?

Constructive criticism generally meets these criteria:

- *It addresses the issue, not the person.* Constructive criticism concentrates on the difficulty at hand, not on the qualities of the person being criticized. It doesn't say or imply that "you're stupid."
- *It is framed as a mutual problem.* Constructive criticism frames the issue as a mutual problem to be solved, not as a problem that the other person must solve alone.
- *It is balanced.* Constructive criticism balances the positive and the negative: "I agree with a lot of the points you made, Beth, but there's one idea I don't think will work."
- *It focuses on the present.* Constructive criticism deals with today's problem; it doesn't dredge up matters from the past.
- *It shows empathy.* The word *empathy* refers to the ability to share the feelings of another person. Constructive criticism demonstrates empathy because it shows you care about how the other person is feeling.
- *It is open to discussion.* In constructive criticism, the speaker conveys the sense that the listener may have a different—and possibly valid—perspective on the situation.

Did you know

Conflict typically varies according to the stage of a team's evolution. Successful workplace teams commonly go through four stages:

1. *Forming*: The group clarifies its goal and its procedures.
2. *Storming*: Conflicting ideas and feelings emerge—about team roles, procedures, and so forth—and the team must resolve these conflicts in order to progress.
3. *Norming*: As the early conflicts are resolved, the team becomes more cohesive. Standards of group behavior (norms) develop, and most members abide by them.
4. *Performing*: In order to reach its goal, the team needs to concentrate on making decisions and solving problems. Here conflicts should once again emerge—conflicts about specific ideas and alternatives. The key at this stage is to find the right balance between conflict and harmony.

Quick Skills

Framing Criticism

The following comments are examples of negative, destructive criticism. On the blank lines, reword each item to make it more constructive.

1. "You're always late to meetings. Can't you get here on time for once?"

   _____

   _____

   _____

2. "That's just a nutty idea. It's never going to work."

   _____

   _____

   _____

3. "If you weren't always so hyper, you'd see we can't rush this decision. There's too much at stake."

   _____

   _____

   _____

4. "Last time we followed your advice, the result was a disaster. Stop trying to insist on your way."

   _____

   _____

   _____

5. "Why don't you let other people talk? You're not the boss here."

   _____

   _____

   _____

6. "You're interrupting, as usual. Let me finish before you butt in!"

   _____

   _____

   _____

Handling Anger

One of the most destructive features of conflict is the anger it arouses. When people get angry, many negative things can happen:

♦ The angry person says unwise things or makes exaggerated accusations.
♦ Other people get angry as well.
♦ Additional grievances are aired, complicating the situation.
♦ Relationships are strained or broken.
♦ Morale and team spirit are undermined.
♦ The underlying conflict—the source of the original problem—becomes even harder to resolve.

You can't always stop yourself from getting angry. But when your anger does flare, how can you handle it so that it doesn't damage your team?

The following seven steps can help you manage your anger constructively:

1. *Accept responsibility for your anger.* However "justified" your anger may be, it is your emotion, no one else's. You are the only one who can handle it.
2. *Decide exactly what you're mad about.* Analyze the source of your feelings, and separate the real problem from minor, insignificant matters.
3. *Be sure you understand the facts of the situation.* For instance, if someone made what you thought was an insulting remark, find out if it was intended that way. Don't jump to conclusions.
4. *Decide whom you can speak to about the problem.* Usually the best person to address is the one at whom you're angry. In some cases, however, another person might be appropriate, such as a senior member of your team.
5. *When you speak up, describe the problem objectively and focus on the goal you want to achieve.* Leave personal recriminations out of it.
6. *Propose a solution that would be acceptable to you and also potentially acceptable to the other person.* "Harvey, I know we often disagree on team procedures, but if you'll refrain from implying that I'm too young to know anything, I'll listen politely to your words of wisdom."
7. *Afterward, reflect on the entire experience and learn from it.* Think about whether you managed your anger in the best possible way, and decide whether you should modify your approach in the future.

> " Anger is like a stone cast into a wasp's nest. "
>
> —Proverb from the Malabar Coast, Southwestern India

Applying the Seven Steps

Think of a situation in which you've been very angry. Describe how you could have handled it better, using each of the seven steps you have just read about.

The situation was:_____

_____

Here's what I could have done and said:

Step 1 _____

_____

_____

Step 2 _____

_____

_____

Step 3 _____

_____

_____

Step 4 _____

_____

_____

Step 5 _____

_____

_____

Step 6 _____

_____

_____

Step 7 _____

_____

_____

Managing Conflict

Assume you've applied everything you now know about giving and receiving criticism and handling your anger. But you're still in conflict with someone else on your team, and the disagreement is not going away. It's serious enough to disturb the team's functioning. How should you deal with this state of affairs?

Psychologists say there are five basic strategies for managing conflict:

♦ *Avoidance:* This strategy involves ignoring the conflict as much as possible. You simply choose not to argue, not to pursue the matter. This strategy is useful when team harmony is more important than the particular area of conflict.

♦ *Accommodation:* You put your own goals aside in order to accommodate the other person. Again, this is an appropriate strategy when team harmony is more vital than the goal you're giving up.

♦ *Compromise:* When you compromise, you try to meet the other party halfway. You give up some part of your goal, and she or he does the same. Neither of you gets exactly what you wanted, but neither of you is completely dissatisfied. Compromise is an apt solution when you think that "half a loaf" is really good enough or when you don't want to spend the time or effort to struggle further.

♦ *Competition:* Competition means trying to "win" the conflict—to make the other party go along with you, regardless of whose feelings are hurt in the process. This strategy can earn you enemies, but it's sometimes appropriate if you're convinced that your way is the only way for the team to succeed.

♦ *Collaboration:* In the strategy of collaboration, both parties work together to find a solution, treating the conflict as a mutual problem to be solved. This strategy offers the chance for a "win-win" solution in which both parties benefit. Because new ideas emerge in the process, the team as a whole can profit greatly.

For important team issues, the strategy of collaboration is clearly the best one. You'll find, however, that it can't be used in every conflict. Sometimes, even if you are willing to collaborate on finding a solution,  the other party isn't. Also, collaboration often takes a good deal of time and effort. You and the other party have to pinpoint the exact reason for the conflict, identify goals that you both share, and think of possible solutions that can satisfy those mutual goals.

Next time you find yourself in a conflict, think of the five strategies and how they might be used. Then make a conscious decision about how best to approach the conflict—for your own good and the good of your team.

Assessing My Conflict Management Strategies

Reflect on a recent conflict you have had, and then answer the following questions:

1. Briefly, what were the competing goals?

    Mine:_____

    _____

    The other party's:_____

    _____

2. Of the five conflict management strategies, which best describes your approach to the conflict? Explain your choice.

    _____

    _____

    _____

3. Which conflict management strategy do you think best describes the other party's approach? Explain.

    _____

    _____

    _____

4. If you had followed a different strategy, would it have changed the other party's strategy? Why or why not?

    _____

    _____

    _____

5. Considering the outcome, was your choice of strategies the right one? Why or why not?

    _____

    _____

    _____

    _____

    _____

GETTING CONNECTED

The World Wide Web offers a great variety of resources to help you learn to handle your anger. Enter the phrase *anger management* in a search engine and you'll find numerous sites.

For example, the American Psychological Association's article "Controlling Anger—Before It Controls You" is available at

http://www.apa.org/pubinfo/anger.html

AngerMgmt.com offers tips and information at

http://www.angermgmt.com/

And Plainsense has suggestions for managing anger and determining your "anger style" at

http://www.plainsense.com/health/Stress/

WORKSHOP WRAP-UP

- Conflict can be either constructive or destructive, depending on how you handle it.
- By developing skills for giving and receiving criticism, you can prevent many conflicts from arising.
- Steps for managing anger constructively include accepting responsibility for it, analyzing the anger's source, speaking about it objectively, and proposing an acceptable solution.
- There are five basic conflict management strategies: avoidance, accommodation, compromise, competition, and collaboration. Each strategy has its uses.

A new convention center is opening eight blocks away, and the owner of Rosa's Famous Bar-B-Q & Fish Joint wants to expand the restaurant in anticipation of more business. She has appointed a team of six employees to come up with suggestions.

Amrita, a young hostess, is asked to join the team, and she's excited by the chance to help Rosa. At the first two meetings, the team members brainstorm, tossing out ideas for bold changes:

- ♦ Purchasing the empty lot in back to build another dining room
- ♦ Opening the restaurant much earlier and closing later
- ♦ Greatly expanding the menu
- ♦ Hiring more experienced chefs

But after these ideas are mentioned, Amrita notices some curious developments. The team members seem to grow nervous about the prospects. Two of them grumble that the convention center may not bring more business after all. Another says that the restaurant is fine as it is, so why meddle with it? A fourth wonders if Rosa will be mad that they are considering such big changes.

Another curious thing is that the team members act suspicious of one another. Jorge, the head chef, hints that the proposal to hire more cooks is designed to undercut his authority. Linda, one of the servers, whispers to Amrita that some people want another dining room because they think she always gets the prime tables.

The team seems to be bogging down. Finally Amrita speaks up: "Listen, people, any change in the business involves risks, for Rosa and for us. But this is a great opportunity for all of us. Let's not let it slip away because we don't trust each other."

What's Inside

In these pages, you will learn to:

Risk Taking in an Organization

As Amrita realized, any organization must deal with risks. There's no progress without some element of danger. New car models, for instance, would never be introduced if companies didn't take a chance that they would sell. New medicines wouldn't be

developed if pharmaceutical companies refused to risk money on research.

Without some risk taking, the best an organization can do is stagnate. Often, in fact, a company that's afraid of risk begins to decline. It can't keep up with the changing marketplace without taking chances. It can't solve problems if it keeps looking for risk-free solutions.

Risk for team members

In addition to the organization as a whole, risk affects team members. In our scenario involving Rosa's Famous Bar-B-Q, the employees stood to gain or lose personally, depending on the fate of the restaurant. The changes each team member proposed might turn out well or poorly for the other members, and the team's performance as a whole ran the risk of displeasing the boss. Still, the team would miss a great opportunity if the members refused to take risks.

The goal should be to assess the risks as accurately as possible and make careful, informed choices. A business team doesn't risk a huge amount of capital on a very chancy proposition. But if the chance of success is, say, 75 percent, the possible gain is large, and the possible loss is easily bearable, most good decision makers would say, "Bring it on!"

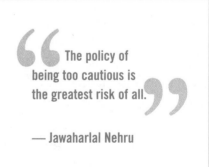

> **The policy of being too cautious is the greatest risk of all.**
>
> — Jawaharlal Nehru

Going to extremes

Each person has a different sense of what constitutes too much risk. Watching a football game with a friend, you may hope your team tries for a touchdown, while your friend is yelling, "Punt!"

The same variation in attitudes often occurs on an organizational team. Ideally, the ultra-cautious people on the team will balance the reckless ones so that the team as a whole chooses a sensible approach to risk.

Frequently, though, this balancing process gets out of kilter. Researchers have found that groups often show either a *risky shift* or a *cautious shift*. That is, when compared to the average original attitudes of their individual members, groups tend to take significantly more risks or significantly fewer risks. The process of talking the matter over seems to push the group toward one extreme or the other.

Why do you think this happens? In some instances, psychologists believe, team members modify their ideas simply because they've heard convincing new information or arguments during the team discussion. In other cases, however, members may drift toward what they perceive as the dominant group view because they want to fit in with the group. They want other team members to like them, or they want to feel a strong sense of solidarity and identification with the group.

This shift toward the extremes—often called *group polarization*—can be a dangerous phenomenon. Luckily, it seems less frequent when the team's decision will have truly significant results for all the members.

> " Progress always involves risk; you can't steal second base and keep your foot on first base. "
>
> —Fredrick Wilcox

Your Attitude Toward Risk

The following questions will help you assess your usual attitude toward taking risks.

1. Imagine this scenario: You have a decent job with an old, established firm at a middling salary level, but you hear of a position you could get with an Internet start-up firm, GnuBizDot.com. If you stay where you are, you'll be secure but not rich. If you go with GnuBizDot.com and the firm succeeds, you could make millions. However, there's a chance that GnuBizDot.com will collapse and disappear, leaving you with no money and no job. Mark the choice you would make under the following conditions:

(a) You are single and have no family responsibilities. The chance that GnuBizDot.com will fail is 30 percent.

    _____ GnuBizDot.com   _____ Current job

(b) The same conditions as in (a), except that the chance of failure for GnuBizDot.com is 60 percent.

    _____ GnuBizDot.com   _____ Current job

(c) You have a family that depends on you for support. The chance that GnuBizDot.com will fail is 30 percent.

    _____ GnuBizDot.com   _____ Current job

(d) The same conditions as in (c), except that the chance of failure for GnuBizDot.com is 60 percent.

    _____ GnuBizDot.com   _____ Current job

2. Analyze the choices you made in question 1 and explain how they indicate your likely behavior toward risk taking as a member of a team.

    _____

    _____

    _____

    _____

    _____

    _____

    _____

Obstacles to Effective Risk Taking

When teams become too cautious, what is it that prevents them from taking appropriate risks? Two broad types of obstacles are especially common: obstacles created by the organization's management, and ones produced by the team itself.

Problems with management

Sometimes an obstacle to effective risk taking stems from management levels in the organization. Team members may feel, for example, that managers aren't fully supporting the team's effort. They may think that management will be suspicious of innovative ideas or intensely critical of failure, in which case it's best to take no chances.

Perhaps one team member is from the boss's own staff. During the discussion, other team members glance at her or him for a signal that the team is doing what it is expected to do, and when this person fails to indicate support, the team becomes wary.

Or, perhaps, after the team discusses a bold plan during one meeting, a couple of team members receive negative feedback from their supervisors: "I hear your team is tossing around some nutty ideas—I'm sure glad I don't have to listen to them!"

For the good of the organization, teams need the freedom to take risks and the freedom to fail. Management should convey the sense that teams are not expected to be 100 percent right 100 percent of the time.

Problems within the team

Sometimes the team has an exaggerated notion of its own importance. The members may feel they are risking the organization's entire future, when in fact their decisions will have a modest impact. In such a case, members may not have done their homework—they may simply not understand the facts about the situation. Or, when the group formed, they may not have taken the time to clarify the team goal and discuss the various options.

Most important, team members sometimes let personal fears get in the way of effective risk taking. Even if management is supportive, the members become overly concerned about being blamed for ideas that prove unworkable or decisions that go wrong. Often this happens because the team hasn't built the kind of group commitment and solidarity described in earlier workshops in this book. Here a key ingredient may be lacking: trust among the team members, a subject you'll read about after you complete Activity 7.2.

Warning! Cautious Team Ahead

From your own experience with teams, recall a situation in which a team made too cautious a decision, refusing to take a risk that in retrospect seemed advisable. (If no business or school situation occurs to you, choose an example from sports, family events, or any other team setting.) Answer the following questions about this situation.

1. Describe the decision and the characteristics that made it too cautious.

    _____

    _____

    _____

    _____

    _____

2. Now think about why the team refused to take chances. Were there outside pressures? Was there a problem with the team process?

    _____

    _____

    _____

    _____

    _____

3. Reflecting on your answers to questions 1 and 2, what lessons can you learn for your future participation on teams?

    _____

    _____

    _____

    _____

    _____

The Need for Trust

The trust that team members feel in each other is a crucial element for effective risk taking. To understand why, imagine what you'd do in the following situations:

- You have a daring idea, but you feel another member is just waiting to shoot you down.
- When you offer suggestions in a team meeting, another member runs to your boss to report what you said, casting it in a negative light.
- Other team members snicker when you speak.
- You try to contribute, but the team leader pointedly ignores you.
- The team accepts an idea of yours and reports it to management. But when management offers some mild criticism, the other team members back away from your proposal.

In situations like these, you would probably keep your mouth shut and commit little energy to the team. And if asked to support a risky suggestion by other members, you'd hardly be inclined to stick your neck out. Why should you exert yourself or take chances for the sake of people who have undermined your trust in them?

Trust is essential before individual team members, and the team as a whole, can begin to take appropriate risks. Trust is also crucial for the aspects of team building that you've read about in earlier workshops: for instance, committing to team goals and norms, sharing work, promoting creativity, drawing on everyone's diverse talents, and resolving conflicts.

Why is trust so difficult?

Trust is a tricky thing to establish, for two reasons:

First, trust is reciprocal—it works both ways. If you don't trust someone, that person likely won't trust you, and vice versa.

Second, although trust generally builds up very gradually, it can be destroyed by a single misstep. You may have ten conversations with a co-worker before you begin to win her trust; but if you then laugh sarcastically at a story she tells, the trust may be gone forever.

Did you know

In a survey conducted by the Franklin Covey Company, 93 percent of the respondents said they believed that their co-workers trusted them. Yet only 81 percent said that they trusted their co-workers.

Three quick ways to damage trust

Psychologist David Johnson has identified three key types of behavior that damage trust in a relationship:

✓ You treat the other person with disrespect or ridicule.
✓ When another person is open with you—revealing personal thoughts and feelings—you fail to reciprocate with personal information about yourself.
✓ Despite another person's attitude of acceptance and warmth, you refuse to be open about your thoughts and feelings.

Two key steps for building trust

As a team member, how do you go about building trust on your team? Ralph Waldo Emerson once wrote that "The only way to have a friend is to be one." In their book *Joining Together*, David and Frank Johnson have reframed the principle in this way: "The key to building and maintaining trust is being trustworthy."

From the moment you begin working with the team, you can take these two steps:

1. Show respect and appreciation for the ideas and feelings of other team members.
2. Be open about your personal thoughts and feelings. Don't gush about them, but share them gradually and appropriately, as the situation allows.

The more respect and appreciation you show, the more you'll get in return. The more open you are, the more you'll encourage other team members to be open. Trust will grow, and when the members trust one another, the team will be prepared to make strong decisions, even if they involve risk.

To see how strongly trust relates to decision making and risk taking, read the feature on the next page about the *prisoner's dilemma*. You may even want to act out a fictional prisoner's dilemma scenario with a friend or collegue.

Trust and the prisoner's dilemma

Imagine that you and a friend have formed a team to rob a bank. You pull off the heist successfully, but then the two of you are arrested. At the police station a mean-looking detective informs you that he's sure you both committed the crime and he's going to give you a chance to confess. These are the alternatives, he says:

♦ If you both confess, you'll both be prosecuted, but you'll get a reduced sentence.

♦ If neither confesses, he'll have to let you both go with just a slap on the wrist.

♦ If only one person cooperates by confessing and implicating the other, that person will go free and the other will get the maximum sentence.

Before you can discuss these options with your partner, the two of you are whisked to separate rooms. You'll have to make your decision alone. What will you do?

This situation is a variant of a classic problem called the prisoner's dilemma. If you can count on your partner not to confess, then you can do the same, and you'll both be fine. But if you don't confess and your partner does, you're in real trouble.

Presumably your regular work doesn't involve robbing banks. But psychologists believe the problem demonstrated by the prisoner's dilemma is relevant in many team situations. The choice depends on what each player thinks the other will do—that is, on how much each trusts the other.

Being Trusting and Trustworthy

To assess how trusting and trustworthy you are, answer the following questions.

1. Of the people you work or study with every day, what percentage do you trust? Mark the appropriate point on the line below.

|_____|_____|_____|_____|_____|_____|_____|_____|_____|_____|

   0   10   20   30   40   50   60   70   80   90   100%

2. Of the people you work or study with every day, what percentage trust you? Mark your best guess on the line below.

|_____|_____|_____|_____|_____|_____|_____|_____|_____|_____|

   0   10   20   30   40   50   60   70   80   90   100%

3. Is there any difference between the percentages you marked in questions 1 and 2? If so, why does that difference exist?

_____

_____

_____

_____

_____

_____

_____

4. What can you do to raise the percentages you marked in questions 1 and 2?

_____

_____

_____

_____

_____

_____

_____

Many Web sites are devoted to the prisoner's dilemma. Some deal with implications for philosophy, mathematics, or computer science. To gain a sense of the wide range of research into this classic problem of trust, enter *prisoner's dilemma* into any search engine.

Some sites offer games or simulations that anyone can appreciate. See, for example:

http://serendip.brynmawr.edu/playground/pd.html
http://netrunners.mur.csu.edu.au/~osprey/prisoner.html
http://www.journey.sunysb.edu/ProjectJava/DiamondThief/

WORKSHOP WRAP-UP

- In any organization—and on any team—progress requires taking some risks.
- Obstacles to risk taking can stem from lack of management support or from the team members themselves.
- In order for teams to take risks, the members must trust one another.
- The key steps to building trust are to show respect and appreciation for others and to be open about your thoughts and feelings.

8 WORKSHOP

Peter and three others form a tight-knit work team for Artown Water Company. They help monitor water quality at the company's facilities. Yesterday they received a report that a child became sick after drinking tap water that the parents said "tasted funny." Today, while another crew checks the child's home and neighborhood, Peter's team investigates the nearby reservoir.

The members do spot checks with field kits and collect samples for detailed analysis in the lab. After several hot hours of work, they gather in the shade of a tree to cool off and discuss their findings. They agree that one trace chemical is showing up at slightly elevated levels.

"Basically, though, this water is fine," says Greg, the team leader and senior member.

"Yeah, I don't see how it could make anyone sick," adds Marisa.

"But we do have this one high reading," Peter says uneasily.

"It's only a little high," Greg points out. "If the lab reports confirm this, we can take more samples next week."

"Right—just stay on top of the situation," Liz agrees. "No reason to panic."

"But should we," asks Peter, "kick around some ideas for finding the source of this change?"

"Sources for minor fluctuations are always hard to find," Greg declares, yawning.

"We could waste days chasing our tails," Marisa chimes in.

"Do we know all the health effects of this chemical?" Peter wonders. "Should we research it? Or check with the state Health Department?"

The other team members, tired after their work, seem content with Greg's plan to take more samples next week, but Peter worries that they've settled too quickly on an easy solution.

What's Inside

Six Steps for Good Problem Solving

As Peter understood, when teams are faced with solving a problem, they sometimes short-circuit the process. Rather than explore new options and discuss them vigorously, the team members may settle for an easy or customary answer. In our scenario, Greg's low-key approach may be fine in most cases, but if there's a genuine threat to public health, the team needs to act more decisively.

People who study group problem solving have identified several key steps in the process. If any of these steps is neglected, the team has less chance of reaching the best solution.

Step 1: Analyze the problem

First, the team has to agree what the problem is. That may sound obvious, but often team members see the matter in such different ways that they are essentially talking about different problems. Imagine that customers have been complaining about one of your company's products, and your team is asked to solve the problem. Some members may see this as a quality-control

challenge ("make our product better"), others as a marketing affair ("stop making inflated claims about our product"), and still others as a matter of customer relations ("pacify the unhappy customers").

For a problem-solving team, defining the problem is a way of clarifying the team's goal. The analysis step should also include determining what resources are available and what further information is needed. If the team needs more facts or evidence, one or more team members should be assigned to collect the data and distribute it to all group members. If the problem is complicated, the team should break it down into various components and analyze each one.

Did you know

In many businesses, most of the information that leads to innovation comes from outside the organization. Think, for instance, of the on-line auctions that have become so popular. The concept of auctions wasn't innate to the computer industry. Most of the background information—how auctions typically work, what people expect from them—had to be drawn from outside the computer field.

Step 2: Set criteria for a good solution

After defining the problem, a second key step is determining the characteristics of a good solution. In our example of the public complaints about a product, is the problem "solved" if the complaints cease? Or if the product is improved so that it passes a certain set of tests? Which tests? What constitutes "passing"?

Sometimes the criteria for a solution can be implicit—that is, unstated but agreed upon by everyone. In this case, it

may be okay for team members to jump directly to the next step in the process. Even so, the team usually needs to back up to discuss its criteria openly before settling on a final decision.

Step 3: Explore alternatives

Rather than settling quickly on the most obvious solution, an effective team tries to identify a number of alternatives for solving the problem. Creative and dissenting views are encouraged. At this stage, many problem-solving teams use the techniques of brainstorming, discussed later in this workshop.

During the exploration process, it's vital for the team to maintain the atmosphere of

trust and risk taking described in Workshop 7. If team members are afraid of being criticized, they won't contribute their most original or far-reaching ideas.

Step 4: Evaluate the alternatives according to the criteria

At this stage the team weighs the various solutions that were proposed in Step 3. Members debate how well each possible course of action meets the criteria established in Step 2. If the criteria haven't yet been clarified, the team should backtrack to do so.

Typically, some alternatives can be dismissed right away because they are impractical, too expensive, or the like. The handful of remaining alternatives may prompt a vigorous debate among team members. Good teams encourage this kind of focused controversy rather than suppressing it. Each possible solution may have advantages and disadvantages, and the team needs to examine these in detail. A good solution is one that can stand the test of debate.

At this stage, too, the team may be able to combine parts of one idea with parts of another, creating a blend that is better than any of the original proposals alone.

> **"** All profoundly original work looks ugly at first. **"**
>
> —Clement Greenberg

Step 5: Choose and implement the best option

After a lively discussion of the alternatives, the team chooses the best available solution. Depending on the size and structure of the team, the choice may be by consensus, with all members agreeing. This is often considered the best way to make a decision, but it does take time, and in some cases it's not possible because some members remain holdouts.

Other methods of making the decision involve some form of voting. Or the team leader, after listening to the discussion, may announce what the majority view seems to be, and in the absence of protest, that may stand as the team's decision.

Some team leaders insist on making the choice of alternatives a two-part process. After the team indicates its choice at one meeting, the leader will schedule another meeting to review and reconsider the decision, just to make sure that significant doubts haven't arisen in the interval.

Sometimes, once the choice is made, the team can simply report its decision to management. Often, though, the team must also decide how to implement the chosen solution. If the team concludes that the best way to improve the quality of steel widgets is to use better steel, then how exactly should the switch to better steel be accomplished? No solution is useful unless there's a plan for putting it into effect.

In many cases, implementing the solution requires "selling" it to others in the organization—convincing them that they ought to go along with the idea. For this purpose, the team needs to summarize the major arguments and decide how to present them in a convincing way.

Step 6: Review the effects of the solution

In some cases, the problem-solving team disbands once it has proposed a solution. If the team continues to meet, however, it should take a further step: watching and evaluating the outcome of its decision.

If difficulties crop up, there may be a chance to revise the course of action. Or, at least, team members may learn valuable lessons that they can apply to the next problem they have to solve.

Problem-Solving Review

Are the following statements true or false? Circle the appropriate letter for each item.

T F   1. The best solution is usually the most obvious one.

T F   2. To clarify its goal, the team should spend some time defining the precise problem to be solved.

T F   3. Though it may take extra time, consensus is often the best way to make a decision.

T F   4. A problem-solving team shouldn't worry about "selling" its solution to the rest of the organization.

T F   5. Once the team decision is made, there's no point in rehashing it.

T F   6. Good problem-solving teams encourage controversy.

T F   7. The best idea may involve a combination of two or more other ideas.

T F   8. If a problem is simple, it's okay to speed things up by skipping steps in the problem-solving process.

T F   9. All the information needed for creative thinking is typically available within the organization.

T F   10. Teams can learn valuable lessons by studying the effects of their decisions.

T F T T F T T F F F

Encouraging Creativity

You've seen how important creativity is to the problem-solving process. In order to select a good course of action, team members first need to be creative enough to propose a number of interesting potential solutions. With dull, unoriginal thinking, the team produces only poor choices.

So what can a team do to encourage creativity? The following sections offer some recommendations.

Brainstorming

To identify alternative solutions, many problem-solving teams use *brainstorming*, the process of tossing out as many ideas as possible without evaluating them. Brainstorming has these characteristics:

◆ The discussion is freewheeling and spontaneous.

◆ All members blurt out their thoughts; nobody holds back.

◆ Even wild, impractical ideas are accepted.

- Nobody criticizes the schemes being offered.
- Group members build on each others' notions when they can, adding modifications and enhancements.
- All the ideas are written down for later analysis.

The goal of brainstorming is quantity, not quality. Often, in the crowd of ideas expressed, there will be a great solution to the problem. Or perhaps elements of two or three ideas can be combined to make that great solution.

Other advice for sparking creativity

In addition to brainstorming, the following techniques can help you foster creative thinking on your team:

- Schedule team meetings early in the day.
- Relax and enjoy yourself, and help other members do the same.
- Assume that you will solve the problem. Banish negative thinking.
- Put aside your preconceptions. Be open to ideas that are "outside the box."
- Don't expect new ideas to be perfect. They can always be refined later. Keep interesting, imperfect ideas afloat awhile to see where they lead.
- Use visual aids to stimulate team thinking: make lists, create charts, draw pictures.

- Use analogies and comparisons to enhance thinking, even if they seem wacky: "This reminds me of my brother's problem with his cat. It went up a tree and didn't know how to get down." "Right! In our case, the tree is . . ."
- If everyone is tired and the discussion is going nowhere, stop work for a while and come back to the problem later, when the members feel refreshed. Researchers say that creativity often requires an "incubation" period.

What Makes You Creative?

You've learned some techniques that experts recommend for increasing creativity in problem solving. But what works best for you? Think about a situation in which you came up with an unusually creative solution to a problem you faced. Maybe you had to figure out how to get a seemingly impossible project done on time. Or perhaps you had a problem with another person and you found a novel way to approach it. Whatever the problem was, answer the following questions about the way you arrived at the solution.

1. How did you identify possible solutions? By brainstorming? By talking to others? By doing research? List any methods you used.

    _____

    _____

    _____

    _____

2. How did you convince yourself to abandon preconceptions and look for unusual ideas?

    _____

    _____

    _____

    _____

3. Did you concentrate on the problem and work very diligently at it? Or did you relax a bit and let your mind drift to other matters? Or did you use a combination of both techniques?

    _____

    _____

4. Looking at these techniques that work well for you, which ones do you think could be applied in a problem-solving group? How much would they help the group?

    _____

    _____

    _____

    _____

    _____

Quick Skills

Groupthink and Other Obstacles

Many teams face common obstacles to effective, creative problem solving. Workshop 7 mentioned one such obstacle, polarization, the tendency for the team to drift toward an extreme position. Two other common obstacles are domination by one individual and groupthink.

Domination by one person

Throughout this book, you've seen that effective teamwork means getting all team members involved in the process, drawing on everyone's talents, and allowing a healthy amount of controversy. Dominance by a single individual can undermine this balance.

What makes a single individual too dominant on a team? Often the cause is one or more of the following factors:

♦ The official team leader may expect, and receive, too much deference from the rest of the group.

♦ A team member with a history of good ideas can automatically win the allegiance of others. If Sukie has always been smart in the past, team members may just go along with her proposals.

♦ If one team member is perceived as an expert on a particular subject, his or her opinions may go unchallenged.

♦ One member may be more assertive than others on the team.

♦ A member may be so loud and aggressive that nobody wants to challenge him.

♦ One member may be highly persuasive in presenting a case, whereas others (whose ideas may be just as good or better) don't express themselves well in a team setting.

♦ A very talkative member may dominate by having the floor most of the time, preventing others from saying much.

As you'll see in the next workshop, handling problems like these is one function of the team leader. But other members should also take responsibility. If you see that one of your teammates is becoming too dominant, for whatever reason, you should speak up on behalf of minority points of view and encourage the silent members to express their thoughts.

Five easy steps to a terrible team

1. Let one member dominate the discussion.
2. Trash other people's ideas.
3. Agree with the majority just to hurry things along.
4. Browbeat dissenters.
5. Act cynical, assuming nothing will ever improve no matter what the team does.

Groupthink

Sometimes team members show an exaggerated, unhealthy tendency to agree with one another, so that everyone's thinking falls into the same pattern. It begins to seem that dissent is wrong or in bad taste. If a member feels doubtful about a team decision, he or she may keep quiet on the assumption that everyone else is agreeing. Or, if dissenters do speak up, others will pressure them to fall into line. Members develop rationalizations for the team's unified point of view, and nobody questions these assertions. Overall, the group begins to think it is smart, invincible, immune to error. Nothing can go wrong because everyone agrees that the team is right.

Social psychologists have dubbed this phenomenon groupthink. It has a terrible effect on problem solving and decision making. Teams that experience groupthink are likely to skimp on every step of the problem-solving process. The chance of a poor decision is very high.

What conditions lead to groupthink? For one thing, it is most common among cohesive groups—that is, groups that are getting along well with each other and feel a strong sense of solidarity. Of course, cohesion is generally good for a team, but groupthink can occur if teams become overly cohesive.

Several other factors seem to encourage groupthink:

♦ A strong leader who promotes a particular solution
♦ Similarity of backgrounds among the members
♦ Relative isolation of the team from the rest of the organization
♦ Strong pressure from the organization to reach a decision

Measuring group conformity

In the 1950s, social psychologist Solomon Asch set up simple experiments to measure group conformity. Each participant was assigned to a group of three to fifteen people. The group was first shown an ordinary straight line. Then the group was shown three other lines and asked to decide which of the three was closest in length to the original line.

The right answers were obvious. Yet Asch secretly instructed all the group members except one to pick the wrong answer. Then he watched the effect of this group opinion on the behavior of the one "innocent" participant.

How much group conformity do you think he discovered? Almost one-third of the "innocent" people's answers were wrong! However, if Asch allowed at least one other group member to pick the right answer, participants were much less likely to be swayed from the truth by majority opinion.

- Lack of established procedures for reaching decisions

If a group starts to descend into groupthink, what can be done to reverse the process? If one or more people are enlightened and bold enough to press for changes, the following steps can help:

- If the team is large, break it into subgroups for discussion and then have these smaller groups compare their results.
- Get opinions and additional information from qualified people outside the team.
- Choose one member to act as a critic or as a "devil's advocate," challenging the team's assumptions.
- Have the leader and other dominant members keep quiet for a while.
- Adopt a formal, step-by-step procedure for making decisions.
- Use secret ballots so that members won't be forced into agreement by social pressure.
- After the initial decision is made, wait for a while and then reconsider it.

GETTING CONNECTED

The World Wide Web has thousands of sites related to creative thinking and brainstorming. Here are a few you can explore:

Creativity Web:
http://www.ozemail.com.au/~caveman/Creative/

The Creative Pages from JPB Creative:
http://www.jpb.com/creative/

Directed Creativity:
http://www.directedcreativity.com/

Creativity:
http://uts.cc.utexas.edu/~barton/mca4.html

Save the Public!

Imagine that you're in a situation like the one described on the first page of this workshop. Your team was asked to investigate a potential public health hazard. The team leader thinks the threat is minor and no immediate steps are needed, and everyone else seems to agree. But you have serious doubts. On the lines below, describe five specific steps you will take to change the team decision-making process:

1. _____

_____

_____

_____

2. _____

_____

_____

_____

3. _____

_____

_____

_____

4. _____

_____

_____

_____

5. _____

_____

_____

_____

WORKSHOP WRAP-UP

- The six steps for team problem solving include analyzing the problem, setting criteria for a good solution, exploring alternatives, evaluating the alternatives, choosing and implementing the best option, and reviewing the effects.
- Brainstorming is a useful technique for promoting team creativity. Other techniques include keeping a positive attitude, putting aside preconceptions, and using analogies and visual aids.
- Two common obstacles to a team's problem solving are groupthink and domination of the team by one individual.

> "The biggest problems in the world could have been solved when it was small."
>
> —Witter Bynner

"Darn it, Miklos, why did you have to get transferred?" Dawn complains.

He grins at her over his computer. "Why, what chaos is erupting in Web Services this week?"

"No chaos yet. But they needed a troubleshooting team for the new Web sites. With you gone, they made me the team leader, and I'm afraid we're going to crash because I don't know how to lead a team."

"Nonsense," he says. "You're ready for leadership. On our teams you were always a leader—you worked hard and you had great ideas."

"But that's different from running the meetings," Dawn insists. "At the first meeting, for instance, I knew we should make our goal clear, but I think I talked too much. I started by telling the others how I defined the goal, and then when I asked for questions, everybody was silent."

"Well, as a leader, you do have to encourage contributions."

"But how do you get people to speak up?"

"With you," Miklos teases, "it wasn't difficult."

"Very funny. But you had a knack for drawing people out. And I remember we had some lively arguments on our teams, but they never went out of control. Somehow you showed us that all ideas could be challenged, even your own, yet everyone's input ought to be respected. I don't understand how to do that."

"Yes, you do. You just explained it. And you know something else, Dawn? From the way you're pondering all this, I'm convinced you're going to be great for the team. All you need is some confidence in yourself."

"But it isn't that simple, is it?"

Miklos grins again. "You're the leader now. You'll have to figure it out."

What's Inside

In these pages, you will learn to:

The Nature of Leadership

Team leadership, as Dawn sensed, can be a complex responsibility. Yet many leadership skills are merely extensions of the teamwork skills discussed throughout this book. If you've learned to work effectively as a team member—if, for example, you support team norms, respect others, and share the glory of team accomplishments—you already have some important skills needed for leadership.

In fact, as you read in Workshop 2, people can act partially as leaders even if they aren't wearing the official leader's hat. One person can become an intellectual leader by proposing new ideas. Another can take the lead in research, bringing in new information. Still another member can be a social leader, promoting group harmony and solidarity. The person who officially heads the team should try to draw out these diverse abilities of the various members.

Is there one special type of person, you may wonder, who makes the best team leader? Researchers have investigated this question for many years. The general answer is "no"—there is no one type of personality identified with good leadership. For instance, some leaders talk a lot; others say little. Some are chummy; others maintain more social distance. Leadership comes in all shapes and sizes.

> ❝ If you set up an atmosphere of communication and trust, it becomes a tradition. ❞
>
> —Mike Krzyzewski, basketball coach

Nevertheless, researchers agree that good team leaders usually meet most or all of the following criteria:

- Intelligent
- Knowledgeable
- Willing to take responsibility
- Highly motivated
- Reliable and trustworthy
- Persistent
- Energetic
- Well organized
- Creative
- Tactful and sensitive to the needs of others
- Tolerant of frustration and pressure
- Versatile and willing to adapt to new situations
- Self-confident
- Skilled in communication

You'll notice that most of the characteristics in this list can be learned or developed. You don't have to be "born" a leader. You can grow into the job, and most leaders do exactly that.

Did you know

The following traits are seldom found in effective team leaders:

- Coldness
- Arrogance
- Harsh manner
- Insensitivity
- Indecision

A Leader You Admire

Think of a team leader you have especially admired in the past. You can choose a leader from one of your own teams or from any team you have observed, such as your favorite sports team. Answer the following questions about this person.

1. What qualities do you believe made this individual particularly effective as a leader?

   _____

   _____

   _____

   _____

2. How did this person acquire his or her leadership qualities?

   _____

   _____

   _____

   _____

3. Of the qualities you listed in question 1, which do you already possess?

   _____

   _____

   _____

   _____

4. What could you do to develop the qualities from question 1 that you don't already possess? Be as specific as possible.

   _____

   _____

   _____

   _____

Tasks of a Team Leader

In today's work environment, the leader doesn't make all the decisions or answer all the questions that confront the team. Nor does the leader dictate the team norms. She or he isn't all-powerful or all-knowledgeable.

What exactly, then, does a leader do?

The leader's basic job is to energize, coordinate, and focus the team's abilities in order to accomplish the team goal. Typically, this involves most or all of the following actions:

- *Chairing team meetings.* Usually the designated team leader will preside over team meetings.
- *Inspiring a team vision.* Vision is hard to define. Basically it involves seeing the big picture, understanding the importance of the team to the organization as a whole, and sensing how great the future can be for everyone if the team succeeds. An effective leader begins with such a vision and manages to convey it to the other members.
- *Establishing a good team climate.* As the one who typically speaks first and directs the initial meetings, the leader has a major responsibility for setting the tone and establishing a climate that reflects commitment to the team and support of all the members.

- *Setting a good example.* In terms of specific group behaviors, the leader serves as a role model. For instance, if he or she listens well, speaks honestly and openly, and conveys respect for all members' ideas, the other members are more likely to adopt these behaviors.
- *Helping the team clarify its goal.* Although all members should help the team clarify and express its goal, the team leader plays an especially prominent role.
- *Empowering and encouraging others.* From the start, an effective leader empowers the other members by sharing power and responsibility and encouraging input from everyone.
- *and development of a schedule.* Sometimes members volunteer for tasks, or the team as a whole develops a way to assign tasks. Often, though, the leader, with the advice and consent of the members, makes many of the choices about the division of labor. Similarly, in developing a schedule, members typically agree on the general time frame, but the leader may need to pin down specific interim dates.
- *Coaching and mentoring.* As team members begin their tasks, the leader offers coaching and mentoring as needed. A good leader reaches out with help rather than waiting to be asked.

- *Coordinating the work of individuals and subgroups.* The more complex the team's task, the more coordination will be needed between different people who are working on different portions of the job. The leader makes sure that members are cooperating and communicating as they need to.

- *Reducing uncertainty and confusion.* In the course of their work, members may reach an apparent impasse. They may become puzzled about what to do next. They may even get confused about their objectives and duties. The team leader often steps in to help the members think creatively and resolve their difficulties.

- *Promoting a healthy approach to controversy and conflict.* As you saw in earlier workshops, controversy and conflict are good for a team—within limits. The team leader plays the primary role in encouraging the expression of differing opinions while maintaining an atmosphere of trust and mutual acceptance. If hostilities erupt, the leader often must initiate one of the conflict-resolution strategies described in Workshop 6. Sometimes the leader plays the role of mediator in a conflict.

- *Controlling troublemakers.* The leader has the primary responsibility for maintaining team norms. If one team member consistently violates the norms or causes trouble, the leader is ultimately responsible for dealing with that problem. The leader may talk to the offending member and if necessary apply some form of discipline. Or the leader may restructure tasks to reduce the troublemaker's interactions with the rest of the group.

- *Recognizing and rewarding positive contributions.* The flip side of punishing troublemakers is rewarding those who make good contributions. Good leaders distribute praise and encouragement widely. By celebrating everyone's accomplishments, the leader builds team spirit.

- *Monitoring team progress.* The leader keeps track of the team's progress toward its goal. He or she reminds people about their objectives and their deadlines. If the team seems to stagnate, the leader focuses attention on the problem and prompts a review of the team's approach.

- *Spurring decision making.* When the team has collected all the information it needs for a decision, the leader often needs to stimulate the decision-making process, prompting the team to evaluate alternatives and choose the best option.

> If you have the desire and willpower, you can become an effective leader. Good leaders develop through a never-ending process of self-study, education, training, and experience.
>
> —Donald Clark

Assess Yourself as a Leader

This activity will help you judge your current potential as a leader and what you can do to improve.

1. Rate yourself on each of the 15 typical tasks of a leader described in the preceding section. Use a scale of 1 to 10, with 1 meaning you have virtually no skill for the task and 10 meaning that you are magnificent. If you haven't yet performed a certain task, choose a rating that reflects your estimate of what would happen if you were given the task today.

    (1) _____ Chairing team meetings

    (2) _____ Inspiring a team vision

    (3) _____ Establishing a good team climate

    (4) _____ Setting a good example

    (5) _____ Helping the team clarify its goal

    (6) _____ Empowering and encouraging others

    (7) _____ Directing the assignment of tasks and development of a schedule

    (8) _____ Coaching and mentoring

    (9) _____ Coordinating the work of individuals and subgroups

    (10) _____ Reducing uncertainty and confusion

    (11) _____ Promoting a healthy approach to controversy and conflict

    (12) _____ Controlling troublemakers

    (13) _____ Recognizing and rewarding positive contributions

    (14) _____ Monitoring team progress

    (15) _____ Spurring decision making

2. Focus on the five items above on which you gave yourself the lowest ratings. For each item, list two practical steps you can take to increase your skill.

    Item number   Steps for improvement

    _____   (a) _____

                 (b) _____

    _____   (a) _____

                 (b) _____

    _____   (a) _____

                 (b) _____

    _____   (a) _____

                 (b) _____

    _____   (a) _____

                 (b) _____

Adapting to the Situation

Researchers who study leadership have noticed that the most effective leadership style often depends on the situation. A technique that works in one set of conditions may not work in a different situation. Most of the research has focused on large organizations or departments, but Paul Hersey and Ken Blanchard have developed a situational theory that is very applicable to small groups.

Hersey and Blanchard distinguish between two basic types of leadership behavior: *task-oriented behavior*, which concentrates on getting the team members to accomplish the task; and *relationship behavior*, which concentrates on building good relations among team members.

Hersey and Blanchard also talk about team *maturity*, which essentially refers to the team's readiness to accomplish its tasks. As the team's maturity level changes, they argue, the kind of leadership behavior should also change.

Using these simple concepts, Hersey and Blanchard describe four leadership "styles" that are appropriate for different stages of team maturity:

1. *Telling.* When a team is new, the members typically need a lot of direction. At this stage the team leader can be especially task-oriented, providing explicit instructions and training.

2. *Selling.* As the team gains experience and confidence, the leader continues to stress task-oriented behaviors but also blends in a large amount of relationship behavior, taking steps to build team trust, encourage openness, and cultivate friendships with other members. Rather than telling the members what to do, the leader tries to guide and persuade them, "selling" them on the approaches the leader considers advisable.

3. *Participating.* When the team becomes fairly mature, the leader can reduce task-oriented behavior and concentrate on team relationships. Team members can work more independently now. Responsibilities are shared. In terms of decision making, the leader may now seem like just one of the gang, no more dominant than any other member.

4. *Delegating.* When the team reaches its highest point of maturity, the leader may fade even more into the background. Now he or she can delegate leadership responsibilities to other members. Even in terms of maintaining team relationships, the leader tends to let other people take over, because they no longer either need or want intrusive leadership.

Not everyone agrees that Hersey and Blanchard's stages apply to work teams. Some business consultants argue that if a team leader starts out by "telling" too much, the team's growth will be stunted, and the members will never learn to think or assume responsibility for themselves. In this view, team leaders should encourage two-way communication from the very beginning and let the team find its own way without explicit directions. Other commentators take the opposite tack, arguing that a team leader should never fade far into the background no matter how "mature" the team becomes.

In spite of these disagreements, one point seems clear: Leadership style isn't one-size-fits-all. As a leader, you have to adapt to the needs of the situation and of the other team members.

ACTIVITY 9.3

Styles of Leadership

Think again about the leader you described in Activity 9.1, and answer the following questions about her or him.

1. According to your observation, did this person's style of leadership change over the course of the team's history? If so, how did it change?

    _____

    _____

    _____

2. Did the team change in its "maturity"—that is, its ability to handle tasks on its own, including such factors as experience, knowledge, and willingness to take responsibility? If so, what were the changes?

    _____

    _____

    _____

3. Did the leader's changes in style (if any) fit effectively with the team's change in maturity? Explain.

    _____

    _____

    _____

4. What does this leader's example tell you about the ways in which leaders can or should adapt to changes in the team?

    _____

    _____

    _____

GETTING CONNECTED

A number of Web sites offer questionnaires to help you assess your leadership qualities. See, for example, the "Leadership Self-Assessment" from the National School Boards Association, available at

http://www.nsba.org/sbot/toolkit/LeadSA.html

Steven Reid offers an on-line test called "Am I a Good Leader?" It can be found at

http://www.globalnode.com/users/stevenr/quiz/

And QueenDom.Com provides a leadership test at

http://www.queendom.com/leadership.html

WORKSHOP WRAP-UP

- Effective team leaders come in all shapes and sizes, but they tend to share characteristics like intelligence, willingness to take responsibility, creativity, trustworthiness, versatility, and sensitivity to others.
- A team leader's many tasks include chairing team meetings, inspiring a team vision, establishing a good climate, empowering others, coordinating the team's work, promoting a healthy approach to conflict, and monitoring team progress.
- Effective leaders adapt their leadership styles to the needs of the team.

Checklist: Teamwork

✓ Teams are increasingly responsible for important decisions in the workplace.

✓ Teams benefit their individual members as well as the organization as a whole.

✓ One of the first steps in teamwork is to clarify the team's goal.

✓ Team roles can be either formal or informal.

✓ Diverse membership helps teams become creative and make better decisions.

✓ For a diverse team to be effective, members need to combat prejudice and stereotypes.

✓ Team norms are behaviors and attitudes that the group considers appropriate for its members. All members help create the norms, and all are expected to follow them.

✓ Willingness to listen carefully is an important aspect of team commitment.

✓ If you're shy about speaking up, four steps can help: identifying the reasons, using logic to refute your worries, keeping your self-talk positive, and practicing these skills.

✓ Asserting yourself requires speaking up firmly, staking your claim to be heard, arguing for what you believe, and at the same time showing respect for others' ideas.

✓ Conflict can be either constructive or destructive, depending on how you handle it.

✓ Steps for managing anger constructively include accepting responsibility for it, analyzing the anger's source, speaking about it objectively, and proposing an acceptable solution.

✓ There are five basic conflict management strategies: avoidance, accommodation, compromise, competition, and collaboration. Each strategy has its uses.

✓ In order for teams to take appropriate risks, the members must trust one another.

✓ The key steps to building trust are to show respect and appreciation for others and to be open about your thoughts and feelings.

✓ Six steps for team problem solving include analyzing the problem, setting criteria for a solution, exploring alternatives, evaluating alternatives, choosing the best option, and reviewing the effects.

✓ Two common obstacles to a team's problem solving are groupthink and domination of the team by one individual.

✓ Effective team leaders tend to share characteristics like intelligence, willingness to take responsibility, creativity, trustworthiness, versatility, and sensitivity to others.

✓ Effective leaders adapt their leadership styles to the needs of the team.

Also in the
QUICK SKILLS SERIES

For information on new titles:
call 1-800-354-9706
or visit us on-line at
www.swep.com